TORCHLIGHT TESTIMONIES

STORIES of GOD'S FAITHFULNESS

TORCH RUNNER
BOOKS

Torchlight Testimonies: Stories of God's Faithfulness
©2025 by Torch Runner Books
Published by Torch Runner Books, an imprint of Harris House Publishing

torchrunnerbooks.com
harrishousepublishing.com
Arlington, Texas USA

Edited and compiled by Megan F.
Cover and interior designed by Gen1 Creative

Unless otherwise noted, copyright in each individual contribution remains with the respective author and is used by permission.

All Scripture quotations, unless otherwise indicated, are taken from the Holy Bible, New Living Translation, copyright © 1996, 2004, 2015 by Tyndale House Foundation. Used by permission of Tyndale House Publishers, Inc., Carol Stream, Illinois 60188. All rights reserved. Scripture quotations marked (THE MESSAGE) are taken from THE MESSAGE. Copyright © 1993, 2002, 2018 by Eugene H. Peterson. Used by permission of NavPress. All rights reserved. Scripture quotations marked (NIV) are taken from the Holy Bible, New International Version®, NIV®. Copyright © 1973, 1978, 1984, 2011 by Biblica, Inc.™ Used by permission of Zondervan. All rights reserved worldwide. www.zondervan.com. The "NIV" and "New International Version" are trademarks registered in the United States Patent and Trademark Office by Biblica, Inc.™ Scripture quotations marked (NKJV) are taken from the New King James Version. Copyright ©1982 by Thomas Nelson, Inc. Used by permission. All rights reserved. Scripture quotations marked (KJV) are from the King James Version of the Bible. Scripture quotations marked (ESV) are taken from The Holy Bible, English Standard Version®, copyright © 2001 by Crossway, a publishing ministry of Good News Publishers. Used by permission. All rights reserved. Scripture quotations marked AMP are taken from the Amplified® Bible (AMP), Copyright © 2015 by The Lockman Foundation. Used by permission. lockman.org.

ISBN (Hardcover): 978-1-946369-14-7
ISBN (Paperback): 978-1-946369-15-4
ISBN (eBook): 978-1-946369-13-0

Publisher's Cataloguing-in-Publication data
    Torchlight Testimonies : a 2025 Torch Runner Books anthology. – First edition.
    pages cm
    Includes bibliographical references.
    1. Christian life—Inspirational. I. Title.
    BV4501.3 .T67 2025
    248.4—dc23

All rights reserved. No part of this book may be reproduced or transmitted in any form or by any means, electronic or mechanical, including photocopying, recording, or by any information storage and retrieval system, without prior written permission of the publisher, except in the case of brief quotations used in reviews or scholarly works.

Printed in the United States of America

To the persecuted Church around the world—
Your faith inspires us.
Your testimonies give us strength.
Your sacrifice calls us higher.

Our hearts and prayers are with you.

TORCHLIGHT TESTIMONIES

STORIES of GOD'S FAITHFULNESS

A Holy Invitation FOREWORD	7
Stamped with God's Image MAX LUCADO	11
Provision PAUL CLAYTON GIBBS	17
The Power of Prayer SALLY BURKE	25
Running Away on Purpose SHARON GAMBLE	33
The Battle for Truth JOANNA K. HARRIS	41
The Awesome in the Awkward MARK NATHAN RILEY	53
The Power of Hope in Transition KAREN SEBASTIAN-WIRTH	63
That Was Our Normal REBECCA FREDERICK LAMBERT	77
Did I Really Say That? PATRICIA HETTICHER	83
Trusting God with My Heart DARIA WHITE OSAH	93
Mess to Miracle JEFF AND ASHLEY HICKMAN	101

Spinning Rejection into Acceptance LAKRISHA COMPTON	109
A Toy Box Miracle TERRY TAMASHIRO HARRIS	119
Though We Sow in Tears KATHERINE WALD	129
The Gingerbread House on Garcia Lane ANNE LEMMONS	137
Honey Bun Surprise LAURA TAYLOR	145
The Mysterious Midnight Ride BENJAMIN SANTIAGO	155
"You Want to Eat at Braum's" RON FAULK	161
The Faithfulness of God to Speak TAMARA J. WANNER	171
A Mentor's Quiet Legacy: Character Over Gifting MARK STERNS	179
The Power at Work Within Us KARI INGRAM	187
My Mary Christmas NANCY CAROLYN LEE	199
Beloved BOB MENDONSA	207
A Note from the Editors	213
Share Your Testimony	215

A Holy Invitation

The Bible tells us that *we overcome the enemy by the blood of the Lamb and by the word of our testimony* (Revelation 12:11). That verse reminds us just how powerful our stories are. Testimonies aren't just good stories—they're declarations of God's faithfulness. They build our faith, disarm fear, and speak life into dry places. They remind us that we are not alone, and that the same God who helped someone else can—and will—help us too.

Testimonies are a holy invitation, not only to those who hear them, but to God Himself, who is waiting for us to come with faith and ask: "Do it again, Lord. Open my eyes to Your presence in my life."

The stories in *Torchlight Testimonies* come from a wide range of experiences. Some are dramatic, telling of miraculous interventions, like the baby rescued from a latrine (p. 207). Others are quiet and simple, moments when God's presence was undeniable in the everyday, such as the one by Max Lucado (p. 11). Each one carries the same weight: evidence that God is personally involved in our lives. He sees. He knows. He cares. And He is faithful. My prayer is that as you read, you'll do more than listen—you'll remember. You'll think of times when God showed up for you. You'll start looking for Him again, maybe in places you hadn't expected. These testimonies might feel like someone else's story at first, but I hope they become a spark that lights your own. And if you've never shared your story before, maybe this book will encourage you to do so. Testimonies carry so much more weight when they come from someone we know and trust. Someone in your life may be waiting to hear exactly how you've seen God work.

Testimonies aren't meant to be kept quiet. They have a way of waking us up to God's presence—not just in the past, but right now. They give us language for faith. And sometimes, your story is the very thing that helps someone else hold on.

Some of the most powerful testimonies come from those who continue to speak of God's faithfulness at great personal cost. Around the world, believers are holding fast to their testimonies despite persecution, imprisonment, and suffering. Their unwavering faith reminds us what it means to truly trust God—and challenges us to live with that same courage. We draw strength from their bravery. It's with deep respect and love that we dedicate this book, and all profits from it, to The Voice of the Martyrs—a ministry that supports persecuted Christians around the world. Their stories remind us that faith is costly, and yet deeply worth it.

Thank you for holding this book in your hands. May it encourage you, challenge you, and most of all, remind you that God is still at work. In every story. In every life. Including yours.

"Jesus Christ is the same yesterday and today and forever." (Hebrews 13:8 NIV)

—Terry Tamashiro Harris, Publisher
Torch Runner Books

Stamped with God's Image

Max Lucado is a pastor, speaker, and best-selling Christian author known for his warm, encouraging style and deeply relatable writing. He serves at Oak Hills Church in San Antonio, Texas, and has written dozens of books—together selling over 150 million copies—addressing themes of hope, grace, faith, and God's enduring love. His work has been honored with multiple awards, including the ECPA Christian Book of the Year, and he is widely regarded as one of the most influential voices in contemporary Christian literature.

Editor's Note: We are deeply grateful to HarperCollins Christian Publishing for granting permission to include this selection from *Unshakable Hope* (Thomas Nelson 2018). Their generosity is a testament to the beauty of Christ's bride coming together as His Church in support of this anthology's vision: to uplift persecuted Christians worldwide through the ministry of The Voice of the Martyrs. Text excerpted from *Unshakable Hope* by Max Lucado (pp. 38-40). Copyright ©2018 Max Lucado. Published by Thomas Nelson. Used by permission of HarperCollins Christian Publishing. All rights reserved.

You have everything you need to be everything God desires. Divine resources have been deposited in you.

Need more patience? It's yours.

Need more joy? Ask for it.

Running low on wisdom? God has plenty. Put in your order.

Your father is rich! "Yours, O LORD, is the greatness, the power, the glory, the victory, and the majesty. Everything in the heavens and on earth is yours, O LORD, and this is your kingdom. We adore you as the one who is over all things" (1 Chronicles 29:11).

You will never exhaust his resources. At no time does he wave away your prayer with "Come back tomorrow. I'm tired, weary, depleted."

God is affluent! Wealthy in love, abundant in hope, overflowing in wisdom.

> No eye has seen, no ear has heard,
> and no mind has imagined
> what God has prepared
> for those who love him. (1 Corinthians 2:9)

Your imagination is too timid to understand God's dream for you. He stands with you on the eastern side of the Jordan River, he gestures at the expanse of Canaan, and he tells you what he told Joshua: be strong and of good courage, for this is your inheritance (Joshua 1:6).

> **You have everything you need to be everything God desires.**

People of the Promise believe in the abundance of supernatural resources. Don't we need them? Are we not prone to depletions? How often do you find yourself thinking, *I'm out of solutions* or *There's no way this will work* or *I can't fix this?*

I recently spent the better part of an hour reciting the woes of my life to my wife. I felt overwhelmed by commitments and deadlines. I'd been sick with the flu. There was tension at the church between some co-workers. I'd just returned from an international trip, and jet lag was having its way with me. We'd received word of friends who were getting a divorce. And then, to top it off, I received a manuscript from my editors that was bloody with red ink. I actually looked for a chapter that didn't need a rewrite. There wasn't one. It was a train wreck.

If you could have read my mind, you would have thought you were perusing the textbook for Pessimism 101. *My work is in vain. I'm going to move to the Amazon jungle and live in a hut. I don't have what it takes to be a writer, minister, encourager . . . human being!*

After several minutes Denalyn interrupted me with a question. "Is God in this anywhere?" (I hate it when she does that.)

What had happened to me? I was focusing on my resources. I wasn't thinking about God. I wasn't consulting God. I wasn't turning to God. I wasn't talking to God. I'd limited my world to my strength, wisdom, and power. No wonder I was in a tailspin.

For such moments God gives this promise: "We are heirs—heirs of God and co-heirs with Christ" (Romans 8:17).

The cronies of dismay, gloom, and dejection have no answer for the promise of inheritance. Tell them, "My Lord will help me. Strength is on the way. The gauge may be bouncing on Empty, but I will not run out of fuel. My Father will not allow it. I am a child of the living and loving God, and he will help me."

> This resurrection life you received from God is not a timid, grave-tending life. It's adventurously expectant, greeting God with a childlike "What's next, Papa?" God's Spirit touches our spirits and confirms who we really are. We know who he is, and we know who we are: Father and children. And we know we are going to get what's coming to us—an unbelievable inheritance! (Romans 8:15-17 THE MESSAGE)

Provision

 **Paul Clayton Gibbs** is the founder and global director of the Pais Movement, a non-denominational Christian missions organization he launched in 1992 with his wife, Lynn, in Manchester, England. Under his leadership, Pais has grown from one pioneering team into a worldwide movement, operating in over 20 nations across six continents, with programs focused on discipleship, leadership development, and equipping everyday believers. Gibbs is also an author whose books and resources—such as *Kingdom Centric*, *The Shapes Test*®, and others—are used globally to help people understand themselves, lead well, and live missionally. Find out more at paismovement.com and harrishousepublishing.com/paul-clayton-gibbs.

When Lynn and I were married, we moved into an area near the church we served. The neighborhood that surrounded us was difficult and rough, so much so that a national newspaper report dubbed it "a ghetto of underprivileged underachievers." As you can imagine, that did wonders for the value of our house.

Over a period of five years, the area became more violent. I constantly broke up fights and, on several occasions, brought bloodied people into our home to bandage their wounds. Because of our low income and my complete lack of handyman skills, our house had deteriorated drastically. Mold clung to the walls, and ice formed on the inside of the windows in winter. We had no proper heating, no double glazing (double-paned windows), and no alarm system.

To cap it all, one night a bad storm blew several roof tiles off our house. Our insurance company informed us that they would not provide coverage because it was normal wear and tear. We would need around £2,000 to fix the problem.

When I shared the vision of the Pais Movement, some of my best friends, who were colleagues in ministry, totally understood the need to reach young people. They even accepted the idea that reaching into schools was possibly the best way to do this. But one of the things that puzzled them was that my wife and I would make the apprenticeships free. After all, funding was tight, and we had limited resources, yet we were committed to breaking down every possible barrier to allow as many as possible to join us in reaching the next generation.

For context, Pais is an organization that equips and mobilizes teams of missionaries to advance God's Kingdom. These teams serve local communities, partnering with churches and schools to create discipleship programs, provide leadership training, and offer creative evangelism initiatives. The heart of Pais is multiplication—raising up leaders who will raise others, all while keeping the training completely free to ensure accessibility for anyone who feels called to join. This meant that, from the beginning, we had to live by faith for God's provision.

Several friends encouraged us not to continue with Pais, suggesting opportunities for well-paid positions at local churches. With a simple phone call, it seemed I could strike a deal with another party where we would both get less than what we originally hoped: I would be doing something similar to what God had told me, and they would hire an enthusiastic, but ultimately frustrated, staff member. In situations like this, especially ones with multiple options, I always default to a simple question: What will most advance the Kingdom of God? The answer to that was straightforward. Difficult as it was, Pais was the way we could most powerfully advance the Kingdom, and, therefore, I declined those opportunities!

Instead, we prayed. I later found out that Lynn even took it upon herself to lay her hands on the walls of our house and pray for healing.

During this time, the tragic murder of Susan, a teenage girl living nearby, shook our neighborhood. During the investigation, the police set up a mobile unit. The heavy police presence over the following weeks caused those involved in criminal activity to move out. Within the space of two weeks, one-third of the residents in that small area moved away. In an attempt to keep what the local authorities called the "respectable residents," they found some European money to pour into the community.

A couple of days after we had prayed for provision to fix our roof, a community worker turned up on our doorstep. He informed us we could get some help to re-roof and a grant for an alarm system. What he said next, however, was particularly interesting. He told us that one street away, residents were receiving grants of up to £12,000. Our neighbors would have to pay 10% toward the costs, but these grants were given in order to raise the standard of living in the community. Unfortunately, we were also informed that our house lay just outside the boundaries for those grants.

We prayed again.

Two weeks later, the local government announced that the boundaries had moved, and we were now inside the eligible area. To cut a long story short, they told us after an inspection that they could give us £16,000 to help with damp-proofing and other necessities. Then, after means-testing us and appraising exactly how much could be provided in grant funds, they told us we would not have to contribute one penny!

As work was done, more issues arose, and then, due to some poor decision-making on their part, they decided to knock the entire house down and rebuild it from scratch. Our home was totally redesigned. The new plan got rid of the mold, installed central heating and double-glazed windows, and, believe it or not, added an extra bedroom. Eventually, they spent £62,000 in the late 1990s. The only original structures remaining were one wall and the floor. Unfortunately, they could not fit in the Jacuzzi I had most politely requested.

Faith is not believing that God can provide; it is no longer dictating how He does it.

Later, we faced another challenge. After six years of living in our brand-new home in a small community of four rebuilt streets, a predictable problem arose. The city council had poured millions into bricks and mortar, but the area labeled "a ghetto of underprivileged underachievers" was just as bad as always. The millions they spent could not deal with the real problems, so the local authorities decided to knock it all down and land bank it. Essentially, the government bought us out, and what they offered was still far less than what was needed to buy a similar house in a reasonable neighborhood.

Had we come to the end of God's promises?

Sometimes God provides by shutting down options. For instance, we were offered an additional grant to help purchase another house, but the house we chose happened to be just outside the area that the grant covered. After looking at many other houses, we finally found a suitable one within the parameters, and no one had bid on it for six months. When we offered to pay a little under the advertised price, a new buyer came along and began a bidding war we could not win. The owner of the house sent a message of apology, informing us that our competitor had offered to pay "whatever it took."

> **Faith is not believing that God can provide; it is no longer dictating how He does it.**

Not long after this door shut, a new and very surprising one opened—an invitation to move to America.

Through a set of peculiar circumstances that included a record-high currency exchange that made the pound almost double the dollar, the low cost of housing in Texas, and some unexpected financial help, we were able to purchase a home beyond our wildest dreams. We went from a small terraced house to a large four-bedroom "mansion."

On my first visit back to the UK, I drove past the last house, the one the bidder had offered "whatever it took." There was no one living in it and no "for sale" or "to let" sign. Instead, a rather peculiar notice simply read: "For inquiries ring this number." So, being the inquisitive type, I inquired.

The house had been bought by a builder who, with a string of expletives, told me:

"I don't know what to do with that house. I drove past it about a year ago, and something told me I had to stop my car and buy it. So I slipped a note through the door, offering the owner anything he asked for it. It is so confusing; I am not sure what to do with it."

It is true to say God does not hide things from us, but for us. The life of seeking first the Kingdom of God has many blind spots, but it is ultimately the greatest view from which to see the world.

Seek first the Kingdom, and He may hide the good stuff from you in order to give you the best.

The Power of Prayer

Sally Burke is the President of Moms in Prayer International. Her vision is that more children, schools, and moms might experience God's life-changing answers to prayer. An international speaker and teacher, Sally is also the author of *Raise Them Up, Start with Praise, Unshaken*, and the *Unshaken Study Guide*.

When my husband and I worked as engineers on the Space Shuttle program, we witnessed how man could defy gravity and reach for the stars. Yet for almost 35 years, I have watched God do something even more marvelous. I've watched Him do the impossible: transform the hearts, minds, and souls of students, teachers, administrators, families, and communities for all of eternity as ordinary women come together in prayer.

Moms in Prayer International is made up of these ordinary women all around the world. As they pray, their prayers touch heaven, unleashing God's power to do His will here on earth.

At Moms in Prayer International, our mission is to

impact children and schools for Christ by gathering women to pray. Our vision is that every school in the world will be covered in prayer. Today, wherever there is a Moms in Prayer group, we are seeing children and schools impacted worldwide for Christ!

Revival Is Breaking Out

In early 2023, I began to see revival and spiritual awakening as we prayed. At a school in Switzerland, 900 students gave their lives to Jesus. Then at Oklahoma University, 59,000 students heard the Gospel, and thousands received Jesus.

In 2024, the answers to prayer continued at a greater pace. At one of our local high schools, a handful of students wanted to do a Christian outreach and were told they could not. So we prayed, and 1,000 students heard the Gospel. After the moms went into prayer again, 200 students in a Christian club at another local high school gave their lives to Jesus.

Not long afterward, I received news from Alabama that hundreds of Auburn students were spontaneously baptized in the lake on campus. At the University of Houston, hundreds gathered to worship Jesus and proclaim Christ as Lord! At Baylor University, hundreds gathered, and when given an invitation to respond to Christ, many repented.

It didn't stop there. Similar stories came flooding in from schools in Florida, Michigan, Colorado, Nebraska, Ohio, Iowa, Indiana, and beyond. A revival lasted for days at Texas A&M. At Florida State University, 4,500 students confessed their sins and struggles and were baptized. Hundreds responded to the Gospel at the University of Georgia, where 7,000 students gathered at Stegeman Coliseum to lift the name of Jesus. Afterward, hundreds of students gathered for baptisms at a fraternity house's parking lot. Then, at the University of Tennessee, at a gathering of 5,500 students, hundreds made a life-changing decision for Christ.

Now, we are seeing it happen again in 2025. I've heard reports that 7,000 students gathered at the University of Kentucky, and 2,000 received Jesus Christ as their Lord and Savior. In Ohio, 2,000 more received Christ in one night. At the Collegiate Day of Prayer, thousands of students throughout the United States gathered together to pray. Internationally, we're seeing similar moves in England, Paris, Italy, Hungary, and elsewhere. God is bringing revival to school campuses around the world!

His Power at Work Through Prayer

At Moms in Prayer International, we have been praying for decades. We have been fervently praying for the hearts, minds, and souls of students, and we are witnessing God answer our prayers in incredible ways around the globe.

Whether it is through one child finding their identity in Christ after surrendering to Him or thousands responding to the Gospel as we have seen, God is impacting our school campuses—and it is just beginning! That is what God does as we pray!

As you read this and think of your own children, you may feel overwhelmed, frightened, worried, anxious, and more. I want to reassure you: our All-Knowing, Sovereign God has placed you right where you live, in this period of time, purposefully! He will empower you to be victorious over your fears, doubts, failures, circumstances, and even the craziness of the world so that you—and your children—can fulfill the great destiny that God has planned for your lives.

> *Our All-Knowing, Sovereign God has placed you right where you live ... purposefully!*

The same God who sovereignly placed you here

has also selected our children and grandchildren. Just as God created Deborah, Daniel, David, Esther, Joshua, Paul, Martha, Mary, Peter, Elizabeth, and others for their moment in history, He has created our children and placed them here and now!

Prepared for Such a Time as This

Daniel and his friends were captured at a young age and taken to Babylon, a pagan empire. They were given new names after pagan gods, were taught at pagan schools, and were thrown into a pagan environment. Yet I believe they were sent forth by God into that nation. They were not conformed to the world. Instead, they prayed, and God used them to help transform the hearts of kings, some of the most powerful and evil kings of history.

I have learned that prayer is the avenue that God has chosen to transform the hearts, minds, and souls of others. I have also learned it can be our greatest weapon, along with His Word, to protect our children and grandchildren. When God wants to move here on earth, He looks for an intercessor upon whom He can place His will (Ezekiel 22). My life has been forever changed by the power of prayer, and I pray yours will be too.

As Jesus said in John 15:7-8 (ESV): "If you abide in me, and my words abide in you, ask whatever you wish, and it will be done for you. By this my Father is glorified, that you bear much fruit and so prove to be my disciples."

We are told in James 4:2c (ESV): "You do not have, because you do not ask."

So may we all ask, and ask big, for our children and the children of the world. God is bringing revival to the world—and He invites us to be a part of it.

Running Away on Purpose

Sharon Gamble is the founder and director of Sweet Selah Ministries, encouraging and equipping women to take time out of their busy lives to "be still" with God, the One who loves them most. A frequent speaker at ladies' groups and conferences, Sharon co-hosts *The Sweet Selah Moments Podcast* and offers encouraging blogs and Bible studies through her website at sweetselah.org. Her published books are *Sweet Selah Moments (Vol. 1 & 2)*, *Give Me Wings to Soar*, *Loved: A Bible Study of the Gospel of John*, and *Held: A Bible Study of the Book of Psalms*. The following story is adapted from Day 29 of her book, *Sweet Selah Moments: Encouragement for Everyday Living, Vol. 2*.

"The most important [commandment]," answered Jesus, "is this: 'Hear, O Israel: The Lord our God, the Lord is one. Love the Lord your God with all your heart and with all your soul and with all your mind and with all your strength.'" (Mark 12:29-30 NIV)

I wake up with the usual battle raging in my head every time it's my day to "run away." My practical side points out all the important things waiting to be done and whispers that a responsible person gets her work done before she takes a day off. My heart side reminds me that the most important thing of all is actually a Person—and I've committed to meet with Him today. The phone rings, and yet another responsibility threatens to pull me back into the ebb and flow of daily living. The pile of bills stabs at my mind. The ever-overflowing hamper shakes its finger at me, "Doesn't your family deserve clean clothes?"

For almost a decade now, I've been spending one day alone with God each month, and I'm still bombarded . . . every single month on that appointed day . . . with mental pictures of all the responsibilities I'm walking away from. Crazy. It's always hard to leave. Always "too much to do." I can't afford a precious running-away day. The temptation to finish work first is strong. It takes courage to pick up my Sweet Selah Day bag and walk myself out of the house and into the car—but I do it.

The worship CD I chose the night before is waiting for me as I start the car and head out. As the music begins, my heart starts to sing. *You did it*, it laughs! You chose time with God over all that stuff at home. Wahoo! The fact that chores await me seems less urgent once I'm on my way. I stop and pick up my favorite chai drink from Aroma Joe's and speak out loud to my King,

"Forgive me, Lord. It's still hard to leave . . . and yet . . . I want to be with You, and I know this is Your will for me. Bless this day, Father, with Your presence and Your words. I give it to You, and I give myself to You. Use me as You choose, teach me as You please, and help me to set aside all else for the pure joy of being 'just us' today!"

And then I sing out loud in the car. And I do mean loud. Sometimes I literally weep for the joy of being free from the normal routines and on an adventure with the Lover of my soul—the Shepherd who wants His lamb close to His heart. With each mile and each song, the tensions from the week seep away. The belief that this time is more important than all else reasserts itself. I'm running away for a day with the One who loves me most, and life is very, very good.

The drive to the ocean is about 45 minutes, just about the length of an average worship CD. I love music. So often it's reduced to pretty background noise, but when I'm on a Sweet Selah Day, every word is heard, every harmony enjoyed. The drive is part of the time spent with the Lord. It's musical prayer. It's heart readjustment. It's surrender and reminder and victory, depending on the song. The worship sets the tone for the day, and it's Just. So. Nice. To sing and focus on God.

What I do when I arrive at the ocean varies. I might sit in my favorite little café and order a pot of tea and toast with homemade marmalade. If I choose to linger in a café that day, my Bible comes out, and I study. Or, perhaps I read another chapter in A. W. Tozer's *The Knowledge of the Holy*, my current Sweet Selah Day book. I underline. I journal. I sit. I wait for God to still my soul.

When the weather allows, I walk a path beside the ocean, admiring waves crashing on rocks and seagulls arched in the sky way overhead. In early summer, beach roses scent the path, and autumn leaves color it beautifully in fall. There are benches along the way. I sit. I admire. I listen. God stills my soul, and we are together, He and I, in the midst of His creation. It's a day with a simple agenda: be with God. Love and be loved. The renewal and the resetting of priorities that transpire each time I "stop" to recalibrate my heart. I love these special days.

> *It's a day with a simple agenda: be with God. Love and be loved.*

Still . . . it can feel strangely hard to run away with God. You'd think we'd leap at the chance, but somehow the noise of life clings to us. Maybe we've come to believe that busy equals important. That stopping is lazy. Or perhaps we secretly think we don't deserve a day like this—as if time with the One who loves us most were some luxury, not a birthright of His children. And for some, the thought of sitting with Him in silence feels . . . unnerving. *What will I do? What if it's just quiet? What if nothing happens?*

The enemy of our souls would love to keep us so busy doing "good things" that we never do the best thing: spend time with our King. After all, the way that we show others that we really, deeply love them is by listening to them, spending time with them, admiring what they've done. That's how we get to know them. This time alone with them is a joy, a declaration of their importance. Jesus said loving God is the most important command. So far from being negligent or lazy, spending quality time with God is obedience to the first and greatest commandment! I've learned that "stopping" is a good thing. It's showing my love for my Beloved in a concrete, beautiful sacrifice of time.

Nowadays, I often find that my day away is too short. But I didn't always feel that way. It took time. Even now, I don't always walk away with profound truths, new and brilliant insights, or spiritual revelations. Sometimes

I just read my Bible, journal my thoughts, whisper "I love You," and am content with that. I simply offer Him my day, fill it with quiet and listening and availability, and allow Him to use it as He sees fit. What God does with my offering is up to Him. In the end, that's what these pauses are about: answering the call of the One who says:

> "Come to me, all you who are weary and burdened, and I will give you rest." (Matthew 11:28 NIV)

The Battle for Truth

 **Joanna K. Harris** served as a missionary in Mexico before enduring over a decade of chronic illness. Through her suffering, God revealed more about His grace and gave her a new ministry through writing. You can find Joanna's books and connect with her on her website: gracepossible.com.

January 1994—The warning signal rang through the early morning quiet, jolting us from bed. The guerrillas were on our missionary base! My mom launched into action, helping us three kids get dressed and trying to keep us calm, not knowing how long we'd have to prepare. Moments later, I was hurriedly buttoning my clothes when someone pounded on the back door, rattling the glass. A man shouted in Spanish, demanding that we open up at once.

With supernatural courage, my mom opened the door and faced two armed men in camouflage clothing. She stood her ground long enough to insist that her children put their shoes on. Then the four of us were herded toward the central building on the base—our gym.

Other guerrillas stood outside guarding the gym when we arrived. I didn't count them, but I did notice a lady guerrilla filming us with a handheld video camera as we walked past her. It struck me as strange and heartless. Inside the building, most of the other missionaries had already been gathered. They stood clumped together, the adults trying to comfort and shield the children. The guerrillas singled out one of our missionary men and took him away. Then one of their leaders rattled off a speech in Spanish, which I didn't bother trying to understand. Finally, after ordering us not to leave the building, they shut the door and left.

Some people were crying, still hysterical with fear. Others were looking around, trying to figure out what to do next. Even with the sound of jeeps driving away outside, we hesitated to speak. Eventually, someone suggested we sing a song. Slowly, haltingly, the words rose from our hearts, built into a chorus, and echoed back to us from the gym walls:

> *In moments like these, I sing out a song,*
> *I sing out a love song to Jesus . . .*
> *I lift up my hands to the Lord.**

Some moments in life are unforgettable, and that one was for me. We'd been frightened, harassed, and threatened, yet here we were singing to our Savior. I know each person there experienced that moment in their own way. I can't speak for them. But I can share that from the moment I left our little house with the armed guerrillas, I was carried by the supernatural peace of God. I wasn't afraid. I wasn't ignorant. I wasn't uncaring. I was graced with the peace that passes understanding.

If you have experienced this divine peace, you know exactly what I'm talking about. If you haven't experienced it yet, no words can explain it to you. It was a precious gift in what could otherwise have been a traumatic situation.

The guerrillas had taken two of our missionary men when they left. Our mission leadership quickly decided we should evacuate. We each selected whatever essentials we could fit in a small carry-on bag, and everyone was shuttled in our small mission airplane to the closest city. We never moved back to our base in the hills. (After six weeks in the city, the decision came from the American embassy for all Americans to leave the country.)

Not long after we evacuated to the city, I ended up in an unwanted conversation with an American Christian who'd never been to our base. I bravely shared how God had given me His supernatural peace through the ordeal with the guerrillas. I stated confidently that aside from missing my home and my horse, I really was okay. I wasn't afraid or worried. However, this person didn't believe me. Then they went on to question other things about my life that I had shared—such as my childlike acceptance and peace at eight years old when my dad had passed away. This adult, a supposedly mature Christian, tried to convince me that I had buried unhealthy feelings, denied what was true, etc., etc. I'll spare you the rest.

By the time I walked away from that conversation, I was livid! I've never been so angry before or since. At fourteen years old, I didn't have the maturity to look at the situation objectively or to understand why I felt so angry. I handled it the best I could under the circumstances. I poured out my emotional storm to Jesus. I talked it through with my mom, and she prayed with me. Then I tried to put the conversation out of my mind.

But the damage had been done.

From that point forward, I changed. I started keeping a tight rein on all my emotions—no more enthusiasm, tears, or anger. I became suspicious of authority. If an adult or leader told me to do something without giving a reasonable explanation, I pushed back. I refused to conform, even when someone meant to exert helpful pressure. And I became critical in my thoughts.

On the outside, it probably seemed like I was still the same teenager. I still loved Jesus. I still wanted to be a missionary. I still studied hard, played sports, laughed with my family, and read voraciously. But I kept parts of myself to myself, not even sharing my true heart with my closest friends.

I wish I could tell you this all blew over in a few months . . . but I can't. For over fifteen years, I lived with these burdens, not even consciously aware of how much I had changed. I did notice and wrestle with the critical thoughts. I prayed repeatedly for God to help me not be critical, but the struggle continued.

It wasn't until my early thirties that the Lord gave the breakthrough. I'd suffered through almost a decade of chronic illness by then (a story for another time), when a well-meaning person told me that my health problems were connected to some sin in my life.

I fell on my knees before the Lord and asked Him to show me if there was any truth to those painful comments. In His grace, God clearly showed me that it was actually because I'd been where He wanted me to be through the years that my health had been affected (first as a missionary kid—parasites and concussions; then on a mission trip—an unnamed virus that caused multiple problems; then serving as a missionary after college—one of those bugs whose name I can't spell). If I hadn't been in those places, I wouldn't have had so many health problems piled on top of each other. But I wouldn't have experienced all the blessings God gave me either.

It was so freeing to hear this affirmation in my spirit from the Lord. But God wasn't done yet.

Jesus led me to ask Him a specific question: "Why am I still struggling with being critical?"

The answer whispered so clearly to my spirit, "It's an overreaction and defense mechanism."

"What does that mean?" Then, similar to Paul's experience, the scales fell from my spiritual eyes, and I saw clearly.

My soul had been critical in self-defense because deep inside, I believed there must be something inherently wrong with me. And that's when the Lord reminded me of that unwanted conversation when I was fourteen years old. A conversation that had made me livid—because it had hurt me so deeply. A conversation that countered my childlike faith with human reasoning. A conversation that should have been affirming but was instead traumatic. A conversation that Satan used to plant the lie that impacted the way I lived for over fifteen years.

> *God showed once again that nothing is beyond His restoration...*

At these unexpected revelations, a flood of emotions washed over me—relief, gratitude, regret, consternation, release, and freedom! Speaking out loud, I declared that I rejected the lie that there was something inherently wrong with me. Then I proclaimed God's Word about me:

> You knit me together in my mother's womb. I praise you because I am fearfully and wonderfully made; your works are wonderful, I know that full well. (Psalm 139:13-14 NIV)

> For we are His workmanship [His own master work, a work of art], created in Christ Jesus [reborn from above—spiritually transformed, renewed, ready to be used] for good works. (Ephesians 2:10 AMP)

> Therefore, if anyone is in Christ, he is a new creation. The old has passed away; behold, the new has come. (2 Corinthians 5:17 ESV)

Yes, I still have a sinful nature, but I am God's unique creation, and I am His new creation in Christ. God doesn't make mistakes. There is nothing wrong with me.

Jesus set me free with His truth!

From that moment, God brought so much healing and restoration in my life. I felt safe to let my emotions show again. I returned to my outgoing, friendly, never-met-a-stranger personality. And I felt lighter and more "me" than I had since I was fourteen.

What an irony, isn't it? I wasn't harmed by my encounter with the communist guerrillas, even with their guns and intimidation tactics. God gave me supernatural peace so that I can tell the story of that experience with complete calm, without my stomach clenching or my mouth going dry. But to this day, when I recount that single, life-altering conversation, my throat tightens and tears well up. Satan's attack and my unconsciously believing his lie resulted in many negative ripple effects.

Does my story make you wonder? What if it's not physical harm we should fear? What if the more dangerous threat is one of Satan's lies?

Jesus said, "Do not be afraid of those who kill the body but cannot kill the soul" (Matthew 10:28 NIV).

Every time I read the story of the apostles in Acts 5:17-42, I marvel. They were arrested, put in jail, and later beaten. But they came away rejoicing! The same with Paul and Silas. They were beaten, put in chains, and locked in a dark prison. Yet at midnight, they were praying and singing hymns.

I used to read these stories and think how amazing the apostles were and how I should try to be more like that. But I was missing the most important piece—that these early Christians had a totally different perspective than most of us do. They didn't seem to fear physical harm. And they loved the truth! To them, the truth was worth a physical beating. They believed the truth, and they continued declaring the truth, no matter what threats were made to their physical safety.

Granted, most of us aren't facing physical harm for our faith. But I know for me, I've been more watchful against physical harm happening to me than I've been against the enemy's lies. I realize now that is the true threat. One lie can impact and affect us far more than any physical damage.

God never guaranteed us complete physical safety on this earth. But Jesus did promise that His Spirit would lead us into all truth (John 16:13). That clearly indicates what God sees as more important.

Thankfully, the same God who empowered the apostles is with us today. He can deliver us from our fears, teach us to guard against the enemy's lies, and strengthen us to be people who live in freedom and share the truth in love.

That's who I want to be.

> But you are a chosen people, a royal priesthood, a holy nation, God's special possession, that you may declare the praises of him who called you out of darkness into his wonderful light. (1 Peter 2:9 NIV)

Note: *Our two missionary men who were kidnapped were killed about a year and a half later. Through the years, stories of miracles that occurred during their captivity have made their way to the families of the men. God did not abandon them, and at least one guerrilla became a Christian through their witness. While we grieve losing them, we praise God for their courage to testify of Him in their suffering.*

Our missionaries never returned to that base. It was left vacant for decades—until, in God's timing, some national Christians purchased the property and turned it into a Christian retreat center. I cried when I heard that news! God showed once again that nothing is beyond His restoration, and He is still working out His plans for good in this world.

*"In Moments Like These" words and music by David Graham. Copyright ©1980 by CA Music. Used by permission.

The Awesome in the Awkward

Mark Nathan Riley serves as Global Training Director with the Pais Movement and lives in Arlington, Texas, with his wife Beccy and their three sons. He and Beccy have more than two decades of experience in missionary work and church leadership in places such as Croydon, Manchester, the North Coast of Northern Ireland, and now Texas. In 2010, he launched *Because You're Loved*, an initiative offering simple tools for people everywhere to share God's love in their daily lives; it has since been adopted for use in youth ministry globally. He also writes, teaches, equips, and mobilizes leaders around themes like everyday mission, adventurous faith, and creative ministry. If you would like to read more from Mark, check out *Because You're Loved* on Amazon or find him on Instagram.

Miracles come in all shapes and sizes, even occasionally through the most unexpected vehicles. Some are dramatic and immediate, others quiet and progressive. When Jesus said, "The kingdom is near," we read incredible stories of signs and wonders. But I am pleased to say that promise wasn't reserved for the pages of the Gospels or Acts, and many of us experience God still moving today.

Several years ago, my wife and I found ourselves in a financial crunch. We'd done everything we could to work hard, budget carefully, and be good stewards of what we had. But despite our planning, a key chunk of income fell through unexpectedly. With rent due and working with a tight budget, we found ourselves up against a wall.

There wasn't enough time to sell something. No opportunity to scramble for extra work. No backup plan. Just a fast-approaching rent payment and an uncomfortable uncertainty. Without trying to sound overly dramatic, I still remember sitting at our kitchen table feeling totally helpless. We did the only thing we could do at that moment—we prayed. Nothing elaborate. Just a quiet, desperate prayer, "God, we trust You. Please show us the way through this."

The very next day, while I was at the office, my phone rang. It was my wife, her voice filled with excitement. "You won't believe what just came through the door," she exclaimed. "A letter from the HMRC (the British tax office). Inside, there was a check covering not one, not two, but *four months of rent!*"

We weren't expecting a refund. We hadn't filed anything new, submitted any claims, or even thought there was money owed to us. Honestly, it felt almost too good to be true. I called the HMRC to double-check, convinced they had made a mistake. The gentleman on the other end was calm and kind. "No mistake, sir," he said. "It's your money. Take it to the bank."

To this day, we have no idea what triggered the refund. But what I *do* believe is this: our Father heard us, and He provided.

More recently, I had the privilege of praying for a gentleman at church and watching another miracle play out. An older gentleman raised his hand for prayer during one of our Sunday services. If I remember his story correctly, he was a passionate ten-pin bowler in his younger days. Years of regular, competitive bowling had taken a toll on his knees, though. By the time he came to us, he was in constant pain and struggled to play with his grandchildren, something that clearly brought him much sadness.

He described the pain as an "eight or nine" on a scale of one to ten. That's no small thing. We offered to pray, not with any particular fanfare or polished words, but simply and humbly—thanking God for His love, for the authority He gives us in Jesus' name, and speaking in faith that all pain would go, and all damaged ligaments, tendons, and tissues would be healed.

It wasn't dramatic at first. He began to bend his knee a little, then looked at me with wide eyes and motioned for me to move out of the way. Then, to everyone's surprise, he started walking—testing the knee carefully, slowly at first. A few more steps. Then he picked up speed. And before we could ask him if he felt improvement, he began running laps around the room.

When he finally returned to his seat, slightly out of breath but grinning from ear to ear, he said, "I haven't been able to run in years. I feel no pain at all."

There's no way to describe the joy of moments like that.

Now, to be clear, I don't pretend there's anything particularly special about *my* prayers. I wouldn't even say I have the gift of healing. Most days, I don't feel like I have a great deal of faith either. I think most of us could do what I did if we're willing to step out. At the same time, I would encourage a certain level of caution around people or ministries that like to make these moments overly mysterious or sensational. Healing doesn't burst forth every time I pray—I've seen unanswered prayers, too.

After living in Texas for over seven years, I visited

England this past January and caught up with a couple I've known and prayed for over the last twenty years.

Early in their marriage, before I knew them, the wife sadly became seriously ill and spent weeks in hospital. Though she survived, her mobility was permanently and significantly affected. She lives with chronic pain and limited movement. Over the years, they've heard story after story from me of people being healed through prayer—stories like Callum's.

Callum was just a teenager when we first met him through one of our school outreach programs. He used a wheelchair due to scoliosis so severe that he was unable to walk. Our team leader, Leo, prayed with him. The next time we saw him, he was using crutches. Leo prayed again. A few weeks later, Callum came in with just one crutch. And not long after that, Callum showed up walking unaided—smiling and getting stronger by the day.

A follow-up appointment with his doctor revealed his spine was straight for the first time in his life. His shoulders were aligned. The doctor was stunned, as was his mum.

And yet, despite hearing stories like Callum's, my friends back in England remained unhealed. But when I saw them this year, they asked me to pray again.

In moments like these, we're faced with a choice. Will we retreat into disappointment? Or will we lean forward in faith, contending for what Scripture shows us is possible? I don't have a tidy theological answer for why some are healed while we still wait in expectation for others. But I do know this: I will keep praying.

Opportunities to see God move are rarely far away. A look around our workplaces, coffee shops, or even the grocery store can reveal echoes of what Jesus saw when Matthew wrote:

> Jesus went through all the towns and villages, teaching in their synagogues, proclaiming the good news of the kingdom and healing every disease and sickness. When he saw the crowds, he had compassion on them, because they were harassed and helpless, like sheep without a shepherd. (Matthew 9:35-36 NIV)

My friend James used to say, "The awesome is in the awkward." He wasn't wrong.

I've lived on mission for the past 25 years and spent much of that time leading workshops on evangelism and discipleship. You might think that by now I would have found a level of peace and comfort with visiting schools or coffee shops to proclaim the good news of the Kingdom and offer experiences of it through healing and signs and wonders. Yet it still takes all the courage I can muster to walk across a room and offer someone an encounter with Jesus.

Each time, I have no idea how it may play out. I worry whether they will be receptive; I worry whether anything will happen; and I worry whether I will be able to articulate God's love in a way that will engage people. I know we're not supposed to worry, but those are all real and honest thoughts I wrestle with.

> *In moments like these, we're faced with a choice. Will we retreat into disappointment? Or will we lean forward in faith?*

That said, only when I embrace the awkwardness and step out—despite wrestling with all those thoughts and emotions—have I had the privilege of seeing God's Kingdom at work in people's lives. And some of them, without my decision to reach out, might never have experienced His Kingdom at work in their lives.

Like the moment I went to pick up my car from a repair shop. When I arrived, the mechanic came out hobbling. "Sorry for the delay," he said, "my knee's playing up bad today."

I was ready to get on with my errands. It would have been easy to nod sympathetically and try to say something to hurry him along so I could get on my way. But something prompted me to share the story of the man at church whose knee had been healed. So I took a breath and asked, "What happened to your knee?"

He told me about a motorbike accident years ago. Multiple surgeries. Chronic pain. Some days—like today—it was almost unbearable.

I asked if I could pray.

Right there, surrounded by the smell of motor oil and exhaust fumes, I thanked Jesus for the love and authority given to us and then made space for Him to heal his knee. Nothing fancy again. Just a heartfelt prayer.

As I prayed, I noticed his eyes welling up. "It's getting warm," he said quietly, "and the pain . . . it's melting away."

He shifted his weight. Then stood fully upright. He took a few steps, then hugged me, overcome. "It's gone," he said, laughing. "The pain's gone."

He walked back into the garage to finish my car. Pain-free.

Moments like this have been an incredible privilege—not because they're flashy, but because they're *real*.

They are windows into the heart of the God who sees, who loves, and who still heals today. Sometimes we see the miracle instantly. Other times, we don't. But every act of faith, no matter how small or awkward, carries the potential to demonstrate the nearness of the Kingdom.

The awesome *is* in the awkward. It's often just one brave, obedient step away.

The Power of Hope in Transition

Karen Sebastian-Wirth, also known as "The Hope Lady," is an ordained minister, author, speaker, blogger, entrepreneur, and longevity coach who shares from the depths of her own journey including seasons of grief, caregiving, and recovery. She delivers messages of hope in a variety of settings—from Fortune 500 leadership training to intimate seminars—and through her *Hope is Powerful* podcast. Among her published works are *The Power of Hope in Mourning*, *The Power of Hope for Caregivers*, and *The Power of Hope for Prodigals*, which aim to help people move from darkness toward healing and confident hope. Connect with Karen at KarenSebastian.com or on Instagram @the.hope.lady.

I woke up from a sound sleep and stumbled toward the bedroom door, which opened to a long, dark hallway. I was looking forward to a strong cup of coffee. I slowly shook my head, remembering last night. Tears formed as I recalled all those who had gathered to celebrate Bill's life.

Sleep had come more easily than it had in weeks now that his life celebration was finished. My days had seemed like a whirlwind as I kept remembering details that needed to be handled so everything would go well.

I paused and chuckled as I remembered the last time we had talked about his wishes for his memorial. Out of nowhere, Bill brought up a subject I did not like to discuss—his funeral. His "earth suit" (as he liked to call his failing body) was wearing thin, and I knew it was on his mind. Death comes to all of us at some point, yet I did not like to talk about the topic.

"You know what? I don't want you to have my service at a mortuary," he stated calmly.

"Oh, let's not talk about that," I replied softly, with a sinking sensation in the pit of my stomach.

"We need to talk about it," he replied forcefully. "I really don't care what songs you sing, because I'll be worshiping my Savior and Lord," he continued. "The reason I don't want the service in a mortuary is that people don't worship. It feels like the focus is on the sad part and not the happy side—that I get to worship my Savior and Lord in my new heavenly body. Promise me you will remember this conversation."

"I promise," I responded quickly, as I abruptly stood.

"And one more thing. No suits and ties. Let's invite everyone to wear their Hawaiian shirts," he continued.

My first step into the hallway brought me back to the moment as I heard the familiar creak of the old hardwood floor.

Bill's celebration of life the night before had been unusual and different, just like he requested. We met at our church, and everyone wore their favorite Hawaiian shirt or football jersey. The kids and I led worship. Men from different stages of his life shared how his life had impacted theirs. A lifelong friend, Don, had us laughing uproariously as he told the story of Bill riding a rotating cross on top of Angelus Temple before we got married. My husband had made his best friend promise never to tell me about it because I would kill him if I ever found out.

As I took another step, my tears began to flow freely as reality sank in.

"Your caregiving assignment is over," I said softly to myself.

I alternated between happiness and overwhelming sadness. I was joyful about the newfound strength and freedom Bill was experiencing as he ran around heaven, praising at the top of his lungs and waving his arms over his head (something he was never able to do because of FSHD—a form of muscular dystrophy). My sorrow was deep as I realized that now my life was going to be totally different after 39 years of marriage. The last two and a half years had been especially hard, since Bill could not swallow, breathe on his own, or get out of bed unassisted. I had quit my job to become his full-time caregiver.

Once I reached the kitchen, I found comfort in the routine task of making a pot of coffee. I sat down to drink it, feeling completely lost because I no longer had caregiving responsibilities. For a couple of years, I had lived with a strict schedule of feeding Bill through a feeding tube.

I didn't know what to do with myself during this transition. When I was out and about, I felt like I needed to hurry home, only to be engulfed by emptiness and tears.

I had a training session to conduct—the one cut short by the news of his death. It felt good to have the chance to see all my friends and focus on their development as leaders. The hardest times were in the evenings because I did not get to have my regular talks with Bill. Still, I was excited to get home . . . that is, until I walked in the door. That's when the emptiness of our home hit me. It was a shell of what it had been before.

As I reached the hallway, I hit the light switch. The light bulb flashed, and I knew it had burned out. I had entered a dark hallway—a time of transition. I had joined a club I never wanted to be a part of... I was now a widow.

Most widows take a financial hit when their husband dies. In our case, this had already happened a couple of years before. Bill had resigned as a church pastor, and I had become his caregiver. For the last two and a half years, I had been by his side as he needed, providing full-time care. He was a very private person and preferred that I be the one helping with personal matters.

I realized that I could now go back to work and soon received an email from a friend recommending me for a special project. I went through the interview process with the owner of the company, and it looked like it was going to be an ideal fit for my skill set. My last interview was with the team leaders who had the final say. I was confident they would pick me.

During my prayer time the night before my last interview, I felt the Lord ask me if I wanted the job.

Lord, this job seems like a perfect fit for me, but most of all, I want You and Your will for my life.

I was shocked when I did not get the job. Then I

remembered my prayer from the night before. It made no sense that this door had slammed in my face when it looked perfect for me in this time of transition.

I felt the Lord say in my heart, "Do you trust Me?"

Of course I do. You are faithful, especially to widows and orphans.

"Then trust Me to bring you some miracles," He impressed on me.

I needed a financial miracle because, as I looked at my budget, it showed a deficit of $300 each month for my mortgage payment.

Answering a Tough Question

It reminded me of a widow in the Bible who came to the prophet Elisha for help when her husband died. Just like her, my husband had served the Lord and been faithful. My children were not about to become slaves, but there was a real possibility of having to do a short sale on my house, where I had raised them.

"Elisha asked the widow, 'What do you want me to do?'" (2 Kings 4:2a ESV, paraphrased).

As I read the passage, I felt the Lord ask me, "What do you want Me to do?"

The question seemed so obvious, yet it remained

one that I had not even asked myself up to this point. I know that God has a special place in His heart for widows and orphans and provides for them in very special ways. Yet, what did I want Him to do specifically for me?

"Lord, I want to see You work in my life so I can testify of Your provision," I muttered as the tears began to flow.

Preparing for a Miracle

As I began to think about the miracles that I had seen during my childhood as a child of missionaries in Latin America, I realized that we had seen many more miracles there than I had recently.

Have you ever thought that perhaps the reason we do not see that many miracles in our lives is that we tend to figure out ways to solve problems without asking and waiting for them? Could it be that the lack of miracles has more to do with the fact that we are so adept at devising solutions that we don't wait for God's timing? What if I took a chance and trusted God to provide supernaturally?

Also, in order to see miraculous provision, I felt that I was not to let everyone else know about my financial need. This was going to demand trust and faith in the hallway of this transition period.

Finding My Personal Worth

The second question that Elisha asked was timely as well: "Do you have anything of worth in your house?" (2 Kings 4:2b NIV, paraphrased).

I decided to dive deeper into the meaning of this passage and pulled out my *Strong's Concordance* (1890). The Hebrew word for "house" in this passage is *bay-it*, which means 'household' or 'family.' The two sons were also part of the story and were an integral part of the miracle.

I looked around at all our stuff and realized I really didn't have treasures to sell on eBay. I held a garage sale that only brought pennies on the dollar for household items.

"What do I have to offer that has value or worth? What is something that only I can do that would have significance and might help someone else?" I asked myself.

As I prayed about it, I felt the Lord nudge me toward expecting miracles as I started once again to write about the power of hope in the years of caregiving and the death of my husband. It felt presumptuous not to work outside the home as I had for decades. Still, focusing on my story and sharing it with others was a true act of obedience.

Discovering the Blessing

"'I don't really have much of anything. The only thing I have in my house that might be of any worth is a jar of oil,' the widow replied" (2 Kings 4:2c NIV, paraphrased).

The second discovery from this study was that the widow had one small flask of oil, symbolizing provision. She was told to borrow as many containers from her neighbors as she and her sons could find. Then, she and her sons were to "shut the door," which signifies surrender. They started pouring, and the oil (abundance) kept flowing. The original flask did not run out until they had filled every bottle in that room.

> *"Lord, I want to see you work in my life so I can testify of your provision."*

Sharing Freely

There was more to it than simply considering the sale of personal items in our home. I realized that this would be the perfect time to share from the experiences of my life. Our family had been through so much together as we cared for an amazing man who had walked through difficult times without losing his sense of humor or faith in God.

I had a container full of the oil of God's presence. We had been through tough times, yet we always had more than enough provision of strength, courage, and blessing. I could share stories of overcoming when I wanted to give up. There had been so many nights when I lay in bed and wept because I was totally exhausted. I didn't see how I could keep going. Yet, the next morning, I had new strength to start the caregiving routine all over again.

I could begin to write about my darkest days and find ways to bless others who find themselves in similar situations. I could share the "hope rays" that showed up just when I needed them and testify of answered prayers in dark times.

Encountering the First Miracle

The miracle of provision for the house payment did indeed come from surprising places.

The next day, my daughters came to our house to help me go through Bill's things. Elizabeth opened the closet and grabbed one of her dad's Hawaiian shirts. She held it up to her nose to breathe in his scent.

"Would you like a quilt made from his shirts?" I asked her.

"He has enough of them to make three quilts—one for each of us," she replied tearfully.

I reached over to hug her as she held out the shirt. My hand felt something in the pocket. We both gasped as we pulled out a wad of $100 bills.

"I was wondering what had happened to our 'emergency fund!'" I exclaimed.

And thus began the series of miraculous provisions. This was exactly what I needed for three months. Here are a couple of examples of other extraordinary miracles:

1. A friend from church had some items that Bill had given him. Without me asking him to do so, he sold them at the best price ever and gave me the proceeds. This took me through another two months.

2. This same friend asked me to dogsit for his three dogs while he and his family were on vacation. He handed me an envelope at the end of that week that covered another two months.

The miracle list goes on. I felt an amazing sense of how near the Lord is to the brokenhearted. We were surrounded by many who loaned us their vessels during that difficult time. They supplied support by sharing their stories of how Bill's loving gift of listening had impacted their lives. The miracles continued for eighteen months, and then, the house was paid off in full.

If you are facing a financial crisis at this moment, take a close look at what is right under your nose. It may not seem like much, and yet, God can multiply it as you begin to share it with no concern about whether or not it will run out. I have seen it in my own life, just as the widow did in Scripture.

God can provide more than enough of what you need, just when you need it, and also give you a testimony to share. As we open our hands and give freely, we make room for His provision and miracles to flow.

That Was Our Normal

Rebecca Frederick Lambert is the author of *Planted: The Revival of You* (Harris House Publishing 2025). Known for her warmth and authenticity, Rebecca lives what she teaches as an author, coach, speaker, and songwriter—that worship is a way of life and we can trust God's redemptive work through every season. Rebecca is co-pastor of The Refuge in Georgetown, TX, and a leader in her school district. She loves spending time with her husband, Jesse, and their two sons, Asher and Gideon. Connect with her through harris-housepublishing.com/rebecca-frederick-lambert.

When I think back on my childhood in Argentina, what stands out most isn't the food or the culture, though I loved both. It's the way the Holy Spirit was woven into the fabric of our everyday lives. He wasn't reserved for church services or big spiritual moments—He was present and active in the ordinary and the unexpected. For us—growing up in the mission field, depending on Him daily—that was our normal.

We didn't use American dollars, and there was no such thing as online banking back then. So from time to time, my mom—yes, we still call her "Mommy"—would have to take cash downtown to exchange it. One particular day, she took a shortcut from our school to the train station, carrying the money she planned to exchange. The path was narrow. As she walked, she noticed two men ahead. When they saw her, they linked arms across the path, clearly trying to block her way.

She didn't panic. She didn't turn back. Instead, she quietly began to pray in the Spirit under her breath and kept walking.

Suddenly, the two men froze. Their eyes grew wide as they looked past my mother, as if something—or someone—was behind her. Without saying a word, they turned and ran. Not just a few steps. They ran until they were completely out of sight.

She never saw what they saw, but later she learned that there had been a string of robberies in that very spot. Whatever those men saw behind her, I believe God sent His angels to intervene. His protection was real and tangible.

Another memory from that time is a bit more personal—it involves me at the ripe age of two and a half. I was a little bundle of energy, running full speed into life, and on this particular day, I was very excited about ice cream. So excited, in fact, that I ran into the ice cream parlor at full speed... and collided headfirst with a steel pole. I was knocked out cold.

My mom and my oldest sister, Brenda, rushed me to the emergency room. When the X-ray came back, the doctor told them I had fractured my skull. The diagnosis was clear, but my mom and Brenda weren't okay with that report. They prayed, hard, and then they asked for another X-ray.

The second image came back clean. No fracture. None. The doctor couldn't explain it—but we could. Jesus had healed me.

Then there's the story of my dad—one that still gives me chills.

My father traveled often to minister in Chaco-Formosa, a region in the north of Argentina that's home to the Toba Indians. He loved those people deeply. On one trip, just as he was about to preach, some locals came into the gathering, carrying a baby. The child was lifeless in their arms.

> **The doctor couldn't explain it—but we could. Jesus had healed me.**

They had already seen the doctor, who told them the baby was dead, but they'd heard about a God who could help. So they handed the baby to my dad and simply said, "You pray to God for him so he will come back to life."

Now, my dad wasn't some spiritual superstar. He didn't have a script for this. He just obeyed. He prayed.

The baby started to breathe . . . then move . . . then cry. My dad handed him back to his mother, and that was that.

Three stories. Three glimpses into the power of God at work in real life. None of these moments were planned. None were orchestrated for effect. Still, each one reminds me of something I hope I never forget: our God still moves. He still heals. He still protects. He still brings the dead back to life.

If these stories seem incredible to you . . . they are. Yet, they're also true, because that's just how our powerful, miracle-working God operates.

He always has, and He still does.

Did I Really Say That?

Patricia Hetticher is the author of *To Cleave*, a biblical historical fiction novel published by WestBow Press. She is employed as an in-home caregiver and volunteers as the hospitality coordinator at her church. Patricia is a wife, mother, grandmother, and Navy veteran.

"I think we should move to Manchester," I blurted unexpectedly, surprising both of us.

It wasn't a thought I had entertained. It wasn't *my* idea. But as I studied my husband's weary face, I knew it was the right thing to do. He had been faithfully commuting to Manchester for 18 months from the humble city of Rochester. We'd raised our family there. We knew it well—like a well-worn coat that felt familiar and comfortable, despite its wear and tear.

"I can find a job anywhere," I continued. "I'm sure the hospitals in Manchester are hiring housekeepers. They are always short-staffed. You can't keep up this pace. I'm afraid you'll have an MS relapse if you do."

He looked at me with concern. "Are you sure about this? You are not a fan of big-city traffic."

"I know. It'll be an adventure," I replied optimistically. "A new start for us after the tough years we've been through."

"If you're positive, I'm totally on board. Start looking for an apartment." He hugged me for a solid minute. "Thanks for being willing to move for me," he whispered.

"For us," I replied.

I kissed him goodbye in the predawn darkness and assumed my position at the computer in our dimly lit apartment living room. It was the third place we had been since selling our house after life went sideways. As I opened the internet, I was on a mission to find the next place we would call home. *Does anywhere in this world feel like home? Aren't we aliens in a strange land, Lord? Lead me on.*

In a matter of minutes, I had found an interesting listing. It was a unique homestead, divided into four apartments. Once upon a time, the weathered farmhouse had been surrounded by an apple orchard. Most of its trees had since been cut down, and the city had grown up around it. Built in 1855, the old monster of a house showed its distress. The front porch roof was propped up with sturdy new beams as it awaited repairs. The landlord's three aged feline friends patrolled the grounds, keeping the field mice at bay. The huge barn that once housed horses was now stuffed to the rafters with the odds and ends of three generations of accumulation. Birds flew in and out of the shattered windows along the sides, and there was a scatter of fruit trees and bushes out back—peach, crabapple, blueberry, and mulberry—their fruits, free for the taking.

At the driveway entrance, two granite posts stood, obsolete and ghostly reminders of the past when horses were tied there while the women stepped up onto a nearby stone to climb into the carriage. I imagined how grand she must have been back in her glory days, this old house, like a bride at her wedding—adorned, polished, and glowing. Her solid foundation and handcrafted framework were a testament to her strength, a strength that had seen her through brutal New England winters, times of wealth, and times of poverty. People came and were gone like the flowers of the field, but she remained.

I texted the phone number and address to my husband, and he was able to meet with the landlord after work. A Navy veteran, he was in his fifties as we were. He insisted I come look at the place before he would allow a rental application to be filled out or a lease signed.

The following day after work, my husband drove home and picked me up. Together, we went and signed the lease. The landlord had listed the apartment on the very day my husband had called. We were the first and only ones to come see the place. Two weeks later, we moved in.

Leaving Rochester meant more than a change in geography. I worked in Rochester as a housekeeper in the geriatric psychiatry locked unit. It was a physically demanding job but very rewarding, and I enjoyed brightening the day of both the staff and the patients.

Many days, I had walked the mile to and from work to allow my eldest son to use my car to get to his job. He lived in Rochester but was no longer at home with us. My daughter was also living in Rochester. Our youngest son—half the time, we didn't know where he was. Our home was a revolving door with each of them coming to stay at some point. A move to Manchester for us would mean they were left to sink or swim on their own. It was a scary thought for me. At the same time, it was freeing for both of us. We could no longer carry the weight of our children's problems. Their faith would have to be tested in the crucibles of life. It would be between them and God now.

I would also be severing my attendance with weekly

prayer partners at a Rochester mom's group. They had been my spiritual and emotional support for seven years, through all the rollercoasters of trauma and illness, both physical and mental. Leaving was bittersweet, and I struggled with feeling conflicted between wanting to hang on and wanting to move on.

Manchester wasn't the type of setting I ever imagined living in, and I had thought we would stay in our Rochester apartment for at least a year. I thought that once I became familiar with the city, we would find a different place, or even buy a house. But God had other plans.

I did not realize how much we needed a fresh start: how dull I had become in spirit. We were wounded. Our marriage had been stretched to the point of almost breaking. Our three adult children were damaged emotionally and spiritually, and, at times, physically estranged from us and each other. We were all struggling to survive and to somehow glue the fractured pieces of our lives back together. *How had it all gone so terribly wrong? How had we gone from a happy homeschooling family to this?*

As my husband and I crawled out of the harshest desert, dying of thirst, we knew we belonged in this house.

It was like us. Damaged, worn, and broken, but still functioning. Here, we could rest. There were no reminders to haunt our days with memories of the ugly, painful past. As we healed, this place became beautiful in our eyes, despite its idiosyncrasies.

We joined a church and built new friendships. The Lord led me to another mom's prayer group where I continued interceding for my children, and eventually, my grandchildren. My husband and I grew closer as a couple, stronger because of what the Lord had led us through. The second year we were here, the Holy Spirit worked mightily in my heart by bringing me to a deep repentance and greater knowledge of Himself. He taught me to see things differently and to walk in step with Him, and I saw with clarity the strengths and weaknesses in myself and my family members and how the spiritual forces of darkness used our weaknesses to sow division and chaos. In His time, the Holy Spirit began mending our wounds with His healing power.

I planted gardens, made jams and pickles, and wrote stories about life woven with emotion and memory. One by one, our children reconciled with us and with one another. Love and laughter resounded once again as we all squeezed in around our candlelit dining room table in the parlor on holidays. We were growing and thriving. I even enjoyed the unexpected reunion with my birth son this past year. His was a closed adoption, and I never even hoped to meet him this side of heaven. But now, he, his parents, sister, wife, and daughter have become an extended part of the family. Truly, God is the One who restores life in all its splendor.

I once viewed ministry as something I do. Now, it's who I am in all facets of my life. *In Him I live and move and have my being.* I am always ready to do the next thing He tells me, like now, when God moved me to be a personal caregiver in a client's home, where I can be the hands and feet of Jesus. I continually wait in expectation for His return when He will make all things new, but I am also grateful beyond words that He did not leave me where I was. I drive through Rochester often to see friends and family. Now, I can enjoy it, remembering the good times and creating new memories.

> *I once viewed ministry as something I do. Now, it's who I am in all facets of my life.*

Life is not without its challenges. There are still consequences and fallout from the past to battle.

But we are no longer trapped under the weight of them. We have moved forward and learned to face them with our spiritual armor on instead of running from them with our backs exposed to the enemy's darts. Ours was a move of body, soul, and spirit planned by Him. He does work all things together for good for those who are called according to His good purpose. We have been at our home here in Manchester for almost nine happy years now. We will be here until His still small voice whispers again or the trumpet sounds.

And when He calls me, I will not hesitate. I will move.

Trusting God with My Heart

Daria White Osah began writing in her teens but officially launched her career in 2018. While she is a fiction author with a deep love for storytelling, she also writes nonfiction and blogs to encourage fellow Christians. She runs an online mentorship program for authors, No Time Writer, designed to help writers reclaim their time and write with intention. Daria currently lives in New York with her husband and family. You can connect with her at notimewriter.com or on Instagram @notimewriter.

"You've always belonged with me."

I will never forget these words, as they were what the Holy Spirit whispered to me during prayer a few years ago. It was the first time I genuinely believed Him, and my heart overflowed with even more love for Jesus. I have had a heart for Christian singles for a long time, and even as a married woman, I hope my story reminds others to wait and trust God's perfect timing. It may sound cliché, but it's true—God knows when to bring the right person into your life.

Before meeting my husband in mid-2021, I had been on a journey of healing with God. Why? Though I grew up in a Christian home with loving parents and best friends as sisters, I didn't have a healthy love for who God made me to be. Being made fun of as a kid and bullied only deepened this struggle. Despite the love that surrounded me—and Jesus' love for me—I found it hard to believe it for myself. The seeds of doubt planted by the enemy took root, and because I was not yet spiritually mature enough to cast down those thoughts with God's Word, they ensnared me.

This led me to seek validation in relationships with the opposite sex. I figured that if a boy liked me, maybe I was worth loving. But this was a flawed belief, and I only drifted further from those who truly cared about me. Even though I had both the love of my heavenly Father and my earthly father, I didn't accept that love as enough. Instead, I dated guys who made me feel like I had to be someone I wasn't. They didn't respect my boundaries, and because I had enough courage to stand my ground, they chose to break up with me rather than honor my standards.

Thank goodness for the foundation of a Christian home. It sustained me when I felt unlovable and as if my life had no purpose. God turned things around in my late teens, giving me the gift of writing, which was born out of an extremely dark time in my life. I entered my early twenties believing I would marry my then-boyfriend, only to experience a painful breakup at the start of my second year of college. Once again, I felt hopeless when it came to relationships.

Thus began my 12-year season of singleness. Yes, there were guys in between, but nothing ever materialized. Their interest always faded. I often wondered if I had "buzz off" written on my forehead, not realizing that God was protecting me from unfruitful relationships. At the time, it didn't feel like protection—it felt painful and lonely. What made it harder was watching people my age in church get married or seeing others compromise their biblical values just to be with someone.

I won't lie and say the thought of compromising never crossed my mind. But by that point, I was too committed to following Jesus. I couldn't give in to what others were doing or believe the lie that my "standards were too high." Deep in my spirit, I knew God had someone specifically for me. I didn't know his name or where he was, but I had to learn to release that desire to the Lord.

I see too many Christian singles settling for relationships simply because they're over thirty, over forty, or approaching fifty. They feel like God has forgotten them. Why would He give them a desire for marriage and not fulfill it? Proverbs 13:12 says, "Hope deferred makes the heart sick, but when the desire comes, it is a tree of life."

So, what did I do during my twelve-year wait? I got even more involved in my church, particularly the music ministry. I discovered God's calling to write and encourage others with my words, especially after He radically changed my life. Even during the height of the pandemic, God nudged me to engage with online Christian communities. I won't say I never felt lonely again, but shifting my focus to my purpose helped me keep moving forward instead of dwelling on what wasn't happening. Little did I know, God was working behind the scenes.

On the weekend of July 4, 2021, I saw a post in a Facebook group that truly ministered to me. It wasn't in my nature to message a complete stranger unless it was business-related, but I felt compelled to thank the man who shared what the Lord had placed on his heart. I wasn't expecting a response, but to my surprise, he replied, thanking me for my message. The next day, he messaged me again, and before I knew it, we were chatting on social media. At the time, he lived in New York, and I lived in Texas, so I assumed our conversation wouldn't go beyond a few messages.

When he asked me to video chat, I felt comfortable enough to say yes. After our second video call, he asked for my phone number, and I knew he was pursuing me. I went from twelve years with no prospects to a godly man pursuing me with intention. I was never confused while dating him, and he never pressured me to compromise who I was. We dated long-distance for a year and four months before he proposed on January 22, 2023. We married on July 29, 2023.

Only God could have brought us together. We had no previous connection—no mutual friends, no family ties. We were complete strangers whom God decided to unite for His glory in marriage. I'm so grateful I waited on His timing because nothing about my relationship with my husband was forced. Everything progressed naturally, and I knew from the beginning that God's hand was on us. Yes, we had to put in the effort to cultivate our bond, but having God's grace on your relationship is priceless.

I share my story with Christian singles who are tired of waiting. Some have never been on a date, some are divorced, and others have never married. Many fear the clock is ticking, that time is running out. I'm here to dispel that lie—God has not forgotten you. He knows your deepest desires, and if you trust Him, He will bring them to fruition.

Is marriage the ultimate goal in life? No, and it's unfortunate that many churches make singles feel that way. They are often made to feel incomplete without marriage and children, but that is a warped perspective.

Our lives are complete in Jesus Christ—no one else. When I discovered this, I became a better person and, ultimately, a better wife. I no longer seek validation from my husband the way I once did in past relationships. I know my worth in Christ, which enables me to love my husband and others even more. I believe my husband is perfectly suited for me, and our loved ones affirm that I am the same for him. Only God can orchestrate that kind of connection—so it's best to wait on Him.

> God has not forgotten you.

I know waiting can feel endless. You wonder, *Will it ever happen for me?* I won't pretend doubts won't come, but remember: you are already victorious in Christ. He has already chosen you. A spouse is a bonus. While I know my husband genuinely loves me, his love is just a drop in the bucket compared to Jesus' love.

"You've always belonged with me." These words will forever remind me of how He healed an insecure girl and transformed her into the woman she is today. Though I still have growing to do, I am whole and complete in Christ—my first love.

Mess to Miracle

 **Jeff and Ashley Hickman** are the founders of Mess to Miracle Ministries, a ministry dedicated to strengthening marriages and families. They believe that the health of the family directly impacts the church and community. With a passion for restoration and faith, they are committed to helping couples and families thrive. You can connect with their ministry at mess2miracle.com.

Jeff

It all began during the summer of 1983. I was fourteen, playing basketball with some buddies down the street. We took a quick break, and one of them showed us a pornographic magazine. That moment marked the start of a long addiction in my life. Through junior high, high school, and even into college, it was a constant stronghold in my life that was set on destruction.

Fast forward to the summer of 2011, when everything came crashing down. It was Thursday evening of Labor Day weekend when Ashley, my wife, discovered what had been going on in my life. At that time, we had been married for 19 years. Beyond the addiction to movies and magazines, she uncovered something even more devastating: I had been involved in six different adulterous affairs over the course of our marriage. Life as we knew it came to a screeching halt. The devastation that swept over Ashley, me, and our children was unimaginable.

Ashley

At that point, I had a choice to make, and my initial choice was to leave. I packed a few things, took the girls, and headed to my parents' house. The plan I had in mind was to figure out how to leave Jeff. I was already planning to ask my parents if I could stay with them until I could get on my feet. I was going to research what school district our girls would be in, as well as begin looking for a job. I had no intention of returning home other than to pick up our clothes. Jeff could have the house and all the stuff. I didn't want anything that would remind me of him. The betrayal was the deepest pain I've ever experienced.

During the night at my parents' home, I was finally alone for the first time after the sordid revelation. In the quiet of that moment, the Holy Spirit spoke very directly to me.

I felt the Holy Spirit ask me these questions:

"Do you believe that I am the God your parents raised you to serve and that you have raised your girls to serve?"

"Do you believe that I am the God who can do the impossible?"

"Do you believe that I paid the price on the cross for all sinners?"

"Do you believe that price was paid for Jeff?"

In an instant, the weight of the price Jesus paid for me came alive like I've never experienced before. I knew God was calling me to return home, embark on the journey of forgiveness, and try to salvage my family.

I also felt a heavy but clear impression: the legacy of our family rested on my next steps, and our daughters needed me to live out my faith in front of them. I understood full well that just because I was choosing to walk in obedience and forgiveness, Jeff might not choose the same path.

Philippians 4:7 became my anchor: "And the peace of God which surpasses all understanding, will guard your hearts and minds in Christ Jesus" (ESV). The Holy Spirit assured me: "I've got you and the girls, no matter what Jeff decides. Walk in obedience and I will take care of you."

With that assurance, I made the decision to return home. I told our girls and my parents, and the next day, we returned to face the brokenness. It was incredibly difficult—every single step was a challenge. It took years of painstaking work before we truly believed we were going to make it, but we drew a line in the sand and resolved to fight for our family.

Jeff

After Ashley chose to come back home, we began intensive counseling. At one point, we were going three times a week—once for me, once for Ashley, and once together. There were so many steps we had to take for me to rebuild trust. That reconstruction was a slow, grueling process, and the recovery came in layers.

I cannot overstate how difficult the work was. We always tell people that healing isn't easy, but it is worth it. God expects us to put in effort, and for us, it included tears, questions, and a resolve to commit to the process regardless of how daunting it was. Our daughters, who were ten and fourteen at the time, also had to learn to love and trust me again. Little by little, God began to transform our lives.

There were so many miracles during our journey,

far too many to recount here. God didn't leave a single area of our lives untouched. From our finances to our emotions, He restored everything that was broken. We were also blessed by family who surrounded us with their support

> **Healing isn't easy, but it is worth it.**

and also by an incredible community of godly friends who stood with us, prayed for us, and refused to let us fall through the cracks.

One of the most impactful and pivotal moments occurred about a month into our healing process. Ashley and I met with a group of ministers, and one of them prayed over us. His words were simple but momentous: "God, we know that this is a mess, and You are the only one who can take this mess and make it a miracle." That prayer planted a seed in our hearts, and over time, it grew into what we now call Mess to Miracle Ministries.

From Mess to Miracle

Our hearts and passion are for marriages and families—to see them restored, whole, and thriving. We want to be a beacon of hope for anyone stuck in a mess. Whether it is in your finances, your health, your mind, your job, your family, or your marriage—every mess is an opportunity for God to perform a miracle.

What God did for us isn't unique to us. He wants to do the same for you—but it requires hard work, surrender, and total trust in Him. The miracle may take years, or it may come in a moment, but God's desire is to never leave us in our mess when we invite Him into it.

Our story is proof that with God, no situation is beyond redemption. It's not just a story of recovery—it's a story of transformation, and with God, *your mess can become a miracle too.*

Spinning Rejection into Acceptance

LaKrisha Compton knows personally how an earthly father's absence—emotionally, mentally, or physically—can lead to fear of rejection in different areas of our lives. Working with other women from similar backgrounds led LaKrisha to publish her book, *Loved and Chosen: A Devotional for the Woman Who Wants to Belong*, to help women discover their identity as children of God, who will never reject them. She is a certified Christian life coach helping women with father wounds find healing and freedom through God's Word. LaKrisha is joyfully married to Dave and is mom to two lovely young women and two fur babies.

Have you ever felt rejected? I have. After all, we were created for connection, especially with God. Yet, several years ago, I couldn't escape the maelstrom of wanting to belong. I didn't understand the depth of that longing at the time; all I knew was that I felt unworthy, not enough, or maybe too much.

One day, I took an online quiz and discovered that I related most to being an "Outcast." That word struck me, but it also marked the start of my journey to fully embrace my true identity.

I began digging into what makes me tick. I realized I'm wired for community—for connection. I crave it . . . yet I couldn't find it. So I joined an online group of women who were also looking for answers for how to overcome their labels. "Outcasts," "Procrastinators," "Rule-Followers," and more—we came together online, sharing our stories and encouraging one another as we learned to conquer our fears and searched for freedom.

A short time later, I sensed God nudging me to write a book—to share my story, to get my message out into the world. I resisted, not knowing how or why my message would matter. After all, I come from a dysfunctional family. Really no surprise there, because families are made up of imperfect humans. But my birth story was especially complicated: I am the illegitimate child of an affair. My mother was the "other" woman to my earthly father, and he abandoned us when I was four years old. That's where the thread of rejection began, and it would be woven through the tapestry of my adolescence and into adulthood.

But God had a purpose for me from the moment He created me. Many years passed before I realized that God doesn't make mistakes and that my birth was not an accident.

I wasn't raised in church, and I wouldn't say that my mother was an outward or obvious Christian. Still, during second grade, I attended Vacation Bible School, and a seed was planted. However, that seed lay seemingly dormant for over twenty years.

During my teens, I felt driven to fill an unidentifiable hole within me. I wanted the attention of a male in my life for reasons I couldn't explain. This led to a life of promiscuity and taking risks that could have ended my life during those years. But even then, God had a plan.

In my early twenties, I got married, and soon after, my husband and I welcomed our first daughter. But life got hard. Military life took my husband away from home for weeks at a time; I didn't have any friends, and I was lonely. Out of concern for my well-being, my husband suggested counseling. That conversation became a fork in the road, and I believe God started gently revealing a new direction.

I learned about a center for new moms at the Air Force Base. Through this center, I found out about an opportunity called a "spouse flight," an event designed to give military spouses a glimpse into their partner's work in the air. Although fiercely afraid of heights, I signed up.

The experience was pivotal—not only because I conquered my fear and fell in love with the plane, such a huge part of my husband's work, but also because I met two other young moms. One invited me to a young mothers' group at her church, which I would soon see was the next step God had for me.

Not long afterward, I joined my new friend at her church, and for the first time ever, I dropped off our two-year-old daughter to be cared for by someone else. I walked down the hall to join the other mothers who were gathered.

When we all settled in, the leader of the group opened in prayer with the words, "Father God . . . ." I don't know what else she said, because those two words lit something in me. The seed planted all those years ago suddenly sprang to life!

Could God be the Father I had longed for . . . searched for . . . *needed* all those years? Could He fill the void I had been trying unsuccessfully to fill for so long? Could God be *my* Father?

I can only describe this moment as a breakthrough, as though Someone flipped on a light switch and illuminated the path in front of me out of a life of fears—of abandonment, of rejection, of being unlovable, of shame, of unworthiness. For the first time, I began to dare to imagine the idea that God could love me, that He could work through me, and that I could be healed. Perhaps more importantly, I began to believe I was worthy of His love and redemption.

I developed an insatiable thirst to know more about God and what He said about me. As I kept seeking Him, a verse I discovered—and still cling to—is this: "A father to the fatherless, a defender of widows, is God in his holy dwelling" (Psalm 68:5 NIV). The more I learned about God as Father, the more whole I felt. That gaping hole in my heart was filled to overflowing by Father God.

Still, doubts lingered. As I sat in church and Bible studies, I sometimes felt God was far away from me. I wasn't sure He knew me. That all changed at a church retreat I attended when I was pregnant. I almost didn't go—I couldn't fit into most of my clothes, and I dreaded standing out in sweatpants while everyone else looked cute and polished.

But I did go, and I'm so blessed that I did—not only because of the wonderful women I met, but also because of what God revealed to me. At the retreat center, I purchased a *New Living Translation Life Application Study Bible* from the gift shop. I carried my new Bible and wandered along a wooded path looking for a place to sit with God. Finding a bench, I sat down.

As I poured out my heart to God, I opened my new Bible. My eyes filled with tears as my gaze took in the words that met me. For the first time that I could remember, I felt truly *seen* and *heard*.

This is what I read:

> "So I tell you, don't worry about everyday life—whether you have enough food, drink, and *clothes. Doesn't life consist of more than food and clothing?* Look at the birds. They don't need to plant or harvest or put food in barns because your heavenly Father feeds them. And *you are far more valuable to Him than they are.* Can all your worries add a single moment to your life? Of course not. *And why worry about your clothes?* Look at the lilies and how they grow. They don't work or make their clothing, yet Solomon in all his glory was not dressed as beautifully as they are. *And if God cares so wonderfully for flowers that are here today and gone tomorrow, won't He more surely care for you? You have so little faith! So don't worry about having enough food or drink or clothing.*"
> (Matthew 6:25-31 NLT, 1996, emphasis added)

Here I'd been worrying about my appearance and wearing sweatpants, but my Father wanted me to know that He had me covered—food, *clothing*, whatever I needed.

My heart burst with excitement that the God of the universe not only knew me, but also cared about what I cared about! To this day, I believe there is nothing too small for Father God to care about; if it concerns me, He welcomes me to bring it to Him. My outlook shifted that day. Far from being distant, Father God came close to me and showed me what I needed at just the right moment. My heavenly Father cared for me.

As my story tumbled out into a book, I grew in strength and resilience. I felt like a butterfly trying to escape the chrysalis that the caterpillar, its old form, had woven around itself. I struggled and I grappled, and when I emerged, I spread my wings as *a new creation* (2 Corinthians 5:17)!

> **For the first time that I could remember, I felt truly seen and heard.**

What do caterpillars do when they spin a chrysalis? They die to self to become something new. I've learned that that's what we must do, too. Every day, every hour, every moment.

Die to self. Die to fear. Embrace our God-given identity.

I want to be like a caterpillar, wrapping myself in God's love through His words every day of my life. I want to die to the self I was yesterday so that I may emerge more and more like Him tomorrow—growing closer to Him and serving the people He brings to me, the way Jesus illustrated over and over again. Jesus experienced rejection everywhere He went, yet He went to the cross to die for you, for me, for all of us who call Him Savior (Galatians 2:20).

We are all worthy, loved, chosen. Our minds, though, try to trick us into believing otherwise. Take a step in His direction. He's there, arms outstretched, waiting for you to come running. And *He* will never reject you.

A Toy Box Miracle

 **Terry Tamashiro Harris** is the founder and CEO of Harris House Publishing and its imprint, Torch Runner Books. Having spent most of her career thus far editing and publishing the works of Christian teachers and authors, she recently published her own debut novel, *Love Remains: A Mercy House Novel*. Connect with her at TerryTamashiroHarris.com or follow her on Substack to see her latest works.

"Mom, where did this come from?" My voice was a mixture of excitement and anxious energy as I examined the tiny calendar I had pulled from my baby sister's toy box.

I had spent most of that summer of 1988 excitedly planning for a move from rural Oklahoma to Boston's Back Bay, where I would be transferring to Emerson College. Hours had been spent poring over the map—studying where my dormitory was in relation to classes and areas in which I could look for work. My dream was to work at a publishing company; I wanted to learn the ins and outs for a writing career of my own.

But first, college. And I needed a part-time job that

could flex with my class schedule while hopefully not consuming too much mental energy. So far, nothing had panned out, and I would be leaving for Boston in only two weeks. But now, here in my hands was a tiny adhesive-backed marketing calendar labeled with the name PWS-Kent Publishing, Boston, MA 02116 . . . the same zip code that would be my new address at Emerson College.

"What is it?" Mom asked, taking the calendar I held out to her as she bounced my little sister on her hip.

"It's from a publishing company in Boston. How in the world would this have gotten in Erin's toy box?"

My mom, a stay-at-home mom at the time for my three-year-old sister, and my dad, a cattle rancher, would never have a reason to be marketed to by a publishing company. My dad had many of the same types of calendars adhered to the file cabinet by his desk or on the dash of his dusty pickup truck, but they had the names of Ada Feedstore or Oklahoma Farm Bureau. I was the one who had been looking up all the publishing companies in Boston—Houghton Mifflin, Little Brown, Beacon Press—but I'd never heard of this one.

Mom examined the company name and contact information. "I've never seen this before." She held it back out to me, but I was already scrambling for the atlas, dog-eared to the close-up map of Boston.

"Here!" I nearly shouted, pinning my finger to the location on the map. "It's right here—just across the Boston Public Garden from 100 Beacon Street, where my dorm is!"

I couldn't believe it. I'd been praying for God to lead my steps. Was this His divine intervention?

"Call the number," Mom said, extending the calendar to me again. "It's okay to make the long-distance call."

In the late 1980s, before I had a computer, and long before Google existed, phone calls were a standard way to find out information, but long-distance calls, billed by the minute, were not cheap. Picking up the receiver of the rotary phone hanging on our kitchen wall, I anxiously dialed the number and waited while the phone connected.

"PWS-Kent Publishing," a crisp, professional voice with its New England accent sounded from the other end of the line.

"Hello, my name is Terry Tamashiro. I will be attending Emerson College this fall, and I'm looking for a part-time job in the area. Can you tell me what type of publishing you do, and would you happen to have any job openings?"

"We are a textbook publishing company," the woman answered, dashing my hopes of entering my dream job, "but as a matter of fact, we do have some part-time positions available. Let me put you in touch with Keri who oversees our drop shipments. Hold, please."

Hold music played while I contemplated my future with a grimace. This didn't sound like my dream job, but I guess my prayers hadn't specified the type of publishing I wanted to be in. Surely, God knew, right?

"Hi, Terry. This is Keri. Anita told me you're interested in a part-time position here." This voice had an even more pronounced Boston accent.

"Yeah—Yes," I stammered, surprised that they were already talking jobs. Keri asked me a few questions about my GPA, typing skills, and schedule, and then told me that she had an opening for a data entry clerk. The job description was to enter ISBNs and addresses to ship books to universities across the States. The work was flexible between nine to five, so I could potentially work around my class schedule.

"Please mail your resume, and when you arrive in Boston, give me a call to set up an interview."

I hung up the phone, stunned and excited. I may have a job! It didn't hold the same excitement as Houghton

Mifflin, but I was thrilled.

Right away, I wrote out a cover letter, thanking Keri for taking my phone call and sharing my keen desire to work in the publishing industry. Then, with a whispered prayer for God's guidance, I sent it off with my resume.

Two weeks later, on my first full day in Boston, I dressed in my most professional outfit and headed over to PWS-Kent Publishing Company. The walk took me straight down Arlington Street, past the Public Garden, where the swan boats glided peacefully across the pond. My heart pounded as I entered the building and took the elevator to their floor.

The interview went better than I could have hoped. Keri was warm and engaging, and after asking me a few more questions about my availability and experience, she smiled. "When can you start?"

"Monday?" I offered, hardly believing my ears.

"Perfect. We'll see you then."

I was hired on the spot! Walking back to my dorm, I could hardly contain my excitement. God had answered my prayers! The data entry job, which some might consider boring, would be perfect for not adding extra stress to my coursework. As a transfer student, I would be taking junior-level classes with extra hours, so twenty hours per week of entering ISBNs sounded blissful. And it would add the needed cushion to my scholarship and grant money.

Yet joy quickly gave way to reality. As I settled into life in Boston, the challenges of living away from home hit hard. Being separated from my family and my boyfriend was harder than I had imagined, especially in those first few months. When homesickness threatened to overwhelm me, I found myself turning again and again to the Book of Psalms. Psalm 139 had long been my favorite, and in that transition, it became my anchor, especially verse 16: "Your eyes saw my unformed body; all the days ordained for me were written in your book before one of them came to be" (NIV).

On the way to work each day, I meandered through the Public Garden. I often stopped to eat my bagged lunch on a park bench, admiring the foliage and letting the antics of squirrels cheer my homesick heart. I thought often about that tiny calendar, reminding myself that God meant for me to be here. I knew He had a plan for my life. Little did I know how perfectly orchestrated His plan was—or how I would continue to be blessed by the miracle find of that little calendar.

I continued working for PWS-Kent Publishing over

the next two years. During that time, I married my boyfriend, and we moved across the Harvard Bridge to Cambridge, where he attended school. Though I commuted into Boston's Back Bay for class, I still enjoyed the blessing of a stroll through the Public Garden each day on my way to work. As graduation neared, I applied for full-time work at publishing companies in the area. I had completed a marketing internship at Beacon Press and hoped that they might bring me on for a paid position. However, my degree in Writing, Literature, and Publishing was with a concentration in writing for children, so I hoped and prayed for a position at one of the well-known children's book publishers. Though I wasn't thrilled about the prospect of working on textbooks, Keri encouraged me to apply for a full-time position at PWS-Kent, too.

After weeks of weighing my options, I reluctantly took Keri's advice and filled out the application for an editorial assistant at PWS-Kent. They quickly offered me the full-time position with benefits, so after exhausting all other possibilities, I finally accepted it. To my surprise, because I already worked for the company, my employment benefits kicked in immediately without having to wait the standard time for insurance coverage.

That little toy box calendar find was still paying dividends, and I was about to find out how much.

Only a month after graduation, my husband and I drove up to Maine to celebrate our first anniversary. I had been feeling a little "off," which I attributed to the transition to full-time work, so a weekend away to picturesque Ogunquit, Maine, was perfect . . . but not enough to shake my symptoms. After noting all possible causes, we made a quick drugstore purchase and then, shortly after, we grasped hands tightly as we watched the little line on the pregnancy test turn pink. I was pregnant! Stunned, my mind quickly cycled through all the emotions—shock, excitement, worry, but then my husband and I looked at one another and laughed out loud. We were ready for this blessing. And, because of that little toy box blessing, the medical care would be covered by my employment benefits. How amazing is our God!

Looking back now, I can see so clearly how God orchestrated every detail of that seemingly random discovery in my sister's toy box. He knew the beginning from the end of my story long before I ever set foot in Boston. Not only was my son's birth miraculously covered by insurance, but I can now see how the "boring" parts of publishing that I learned through dealing with textbook authors and ISBNs would later come in handy for starting my own independent book publishing company. That little calendar wasn't just a coincidence—it was God's perfect timing and provision, placed exactly where I would find it. The same God who knows the number of hairs on our heads had already written all my days in His book. Every step, every need, every provision was planned with perfect love and wisdom. What seemed like a simple job opportunity was actually the foundation for so much more.

> *Every step, every need, every provision was planned with perfect love and wisdom.*

Sometimes God's miracles are difficult to recognize. They can be easily overlooked or forgotten. Yet, God wastes nothing. It's good to take stock, look back, and think about how God works everything together for our good—even the tiniest things, like a tiny calendar tucked away in a toddler's toy box.

He who began a good work in us will be faithful to complete it, one perfectly orchestrated step at a time.

Though We Sow in Tears

Katherine Wald has supported the publication of works from Christian authors for many years and is now stepping into opportunities to write her own pieces. She is passionate about God's mission to the world and hopes her words will inspire faith in others and draw them closer to the Lord.

It was dusk, and my team and I had just returned from a long day of ministering out in the city and the tropical heat. I was sitting in the pool outside our apartment, allowing the water to cool my body and calm my heightened nerves. I had returned feeling more weathered and worn than usual, with a chest so heavy I felt as if a panic attack was coming on. I had been carrying a mountain of emotions most of the day, but had been forcefully pushing them down. Upon returning, I knew I needed space—to settle my nervous system, and to sit and pray.

I was about a month into a couple-month trip on the other side of the world. This was my first mission trip and my first time out of the States. But culture shock, physical fatigue, and shaky team dynamics weren't the things weighing on my mind at that particular point in time.

Before leaving, I had been dating someone I thought I would marry. Marrying a man who was pursuing God into long-term ministry had been a dream of mine, and this man seemed to fit the bill. I deeply loved him, and though he had his flaws, I was giddy about the possibility of doing ministry with him in Latin America and growing a family together. I had even been freshening up my Spanish in preparation for the life I thought was ahead of me.

But things, even from the beginning of our relationship, had been rocky, and through the gentle counsel of a concerned friend, I realized that this man was not the person I should marry. This was a hard pill to swallow, but my loving friend had the foresight to see what this "deer in headlights" could not.

So, I made the hard decision to end the relationship . . . four days before I was to head abroad.

Looking back, I still believe it was the right thing to do, and I'm so thankful for my friend who helped me see that it was necessary. But in that moment, being in a land that was foreign to me and separated from friends and family by thousands of miles, I was heartbroken and emotionally crushed. I grieved the death of the life I had dreamed of while still trying to be present for the work before me.

Sitting in the pool water in the quiet of the evening, my nerves calmed down. But the core, underlying pain remained, and I sat there, very still—not quite numb, but almost paralyzed by grief. Realizing the gravity of where my emotions were, I knew I needed a breakthrough . . . or I might not be able to make it through the rest of the trip.

"Lord," I started, whispering softly, "You've already shown me so much love and grace by what you have given—breath to my body, the beauty of your creation, life in Christ . . ." I paused, tears welling up in my eyes. "But I'd really love to see Your compassion right now. I feel like I'm bleeding out, and I don't know how I can move forward."

My request of God in that moment sounds as if I believe He does the bare minimum for His children. I know that not to be true, having seen Him give grace over and over through many seasons of my life. But my feeble heart, wanting to protect itself, prepared for the possibility of God's silence. I didn't doubt His goodness, but I feared the ache of waiting without hearing.

In the quiet of the evening, as water lapped gently around me and the palm leaves swayed in the breeze, I waited for several minutes, hoping He would speak something into my spirit.

Silence.

There was a flicker of disappointment, but eventually, a reluctant acceptance. I would just have to wait a while longer and bear the pain with the strength He'd given for the day.

After a little while, the sun dipped below the horizon, the stars emerged, and I decided it was time to return to our team's apartment and try to sleep.

After getting ready for bed, I lay down on the mattress, staring up at the ceiling. In the quiet, as my teammates soundly slept in their rooms, I remember feeling the urge to pray again, asking the Lord once again that I might see Him comfort me in the midst of my sorrow.

As I prayed, Psalm 126 flashed in my mind. I didn't know what that psalm said, but the title was clear and unmistakable in my mind's eye.

Skeptical, but desperate nonetheless, I opened my Bible and read the psalm. The last two verses seemed to leap off the page:

Those who sow with tears will reap with songs of joy.

> Those who go out weeping, carrying seed to sow, will return with songs of joy, carrying sheaves with them.
> (vv. 5-6 NIV)

As I closed my Bible, the pressure in my chest dissipated. Tears flowed freely as emotion filled my heart again, but this time, not as grief, but as fierce hope. My pain—and the pain of all believers in a broken world—wouldn't last forever. *Joy was ahead.*

This is your compassion, Father, I said in my heart. *Thank you.*

Not long after, I began to drift off to sleep. Though I still felt grief, my spirit had been filled anew with hope as I clung to this promise: Though I sow in tears, I *will* reap with songs of joy.

Looking back, I don't know why God didn't answer me when I asked the first time. Maybe He wanted me to keep asking, like the persistent widow before the judge in Luke 18:1-8. Maybe He wanted my heart to settle down a bit more so that I could receive more wholly what He wanted to provide. Maybe He just wanted me to be somewhere where I could grab

> **Tears flowed freely as emotion filled my heart again, but this time, not as grief, but as fierce hope.**

my Bible. I don't know—but I do know this:

God answered my cry. He showed me His compassion by reminding me that the pain would not last forever; joy would come. And I now get to carry that memory with me as a gift and a testimony of His deep care for and unending faithfulness to His hurting child.

And I hope, beloved, that this will serve as a reminder for you, too.

Though we sow in tears, we *will* reap with songs of joy.

The Gingerbread House on Garcia Lane

 **Anne Lemmons**, a long-time resident of Arlington, Texas, attends Central Bible Church, formerly Pantego Bible Church. She graduated from the University of Texas at Arlington, where she received a BA with a major in psychology and a minor in English. In 2016, she retired from Alan Plummer Associates, Inc., where she worked for 35 years

---

Upon returning home from my developmental psychology class one summer evening, my sister Charlene announced matter-of-factly, "It happened."

"What happened?" I asked.

"Aunt Gertie has to move. J. Fred sold the farm. She called tonight and asked us to help her move."

Although this news came as no surprise to Charlene and me, Gertie's world was shaken. She had lived on this farm with her husband, Morris, for 32 years. Since his death four years earlier, she continued to live there, where she fed young calves to supplement her fixed income.

The following Saturday, the three of us began the search for a new home. We drove from town to town in the metroplex area, looking for just the right place. Realizing right away it would not be a simple task, I asked the Lord for wisdom. As we kept scanning the classified ads and making appointments, discouragement set in.

Not only did the house have to be affordable, but Gertie had her own list of requirements.

"I want to keep my refrigerator-freezer," she insisted. She wanted to be able to drive, to be near family, and, most importantly, she needed to be able to afford the rent on her fixed income.

Of course, most apartments were furnished with a refrigerator but had no room for a freezer. Gertie had lived in the country all of her 68 years, and she was not accustomed to driving in a congested city. With Aunt Gertie loose on the freeway, we wondered what might happen. Furthermore, in an inflated economy, affordable houses and apartments were in less-than-satisfactory condition.

We applied for financial assistance through the housing office in the city where Charlene and I lived, and the briskly efficient clerk placed Gertie's name on the waiting list. Not knowing when her name might come up for an interview, we continued our search.

It seemed there was no solution. In desperation, I presented her specific needs to my heavenly Father.

Two weeks after we set out to find this "needle in a haystack," we spent all day going from one rundown apartment to another. By mid-afternoon, we were very disheartened. When we got home, I picked up the *Fort Worth Star-Telegram* and listlessly scanned the classified ads one more time.

Then I saw it! ". . . 5-room house in the country . . ." I snapped to attention in my easy chair. It seemed too good to be true, too good to be affordable. Yet, I called to inquire about it.

What a refreshing sight it was—that little ginger-colored house on the knoll near Kennedale that scorching July afternoon in Texas. Best of all, it was an answer to prayer!

"I think I've found you a place to live!" I exclaimed to Aunt Gertie that day on the phone after Mrs. Glady had shown me the cute little brown house in the country. After Gertie saw it, I helped her weigh the decision. I asked myself, "Is this the place?" Wasn't it an answer to prayer? It met all the criteria of my specific prayer request on her behalf. Should I put up the $150 deposit even though she was not convinced?

As I continued to struggle, the words from Matthew 7:9-11 came to mind:

> "Or what man is there of you whom, if his son asked bread, will he give him a stone? Or if he asks a fish, will he give him a serpent? If ye then, being evil, know how to give good gifts unto your children, how much more shall your Father which is in heaven give good things to them that ask him?" (KJV)

I had asked my heavenly Father to provide; and, according to His nature, He would not give me "a stone."

I paid the deposit. We scheduled the move and made arrangements for her utilities. Details were falling into place.

Then, on Tuesday before the move, the housing assistance office called. Gertie's name had come up on the list for rental assistance, and she was invited for an interview. What should we do? Was this additional income crucial for her future well-being? If so, it would mean undoing all the plans we had made and starting over to locate a new place in town.

Indecision.

Turmoil.

Uncertainty.

When everything had seemed to be settled, suddenly Gertie and I were thrown into a tailspin. She didn't know what to do. I didn't know. Hurriedly, I called my friend Peggy and recounted what had taken place. "Let me pray about it," she said. Fifteen minutes later, she called back. "Anne, God is a God of peace. I think you should continue with your move as planned."

"You're right!" I said. "God is not the author of confusion." Recognizing this truth from 1 Corinthians 14:33 and believing God had led us to the "gingerbread house," we decided to move forward as planned. The internal debate ended, and peace reigned.

With help from family and friends, the move went as scheduled, and Gertie was soon settled in. Not only had God provided the specific needs I had requested, but we soon discovered He had also provided extra blessings. Mr. Glady, Gertie's landlord, mowed her lawn regularly and plowed her garden every year thereafter. She soon became reacquainted with a former neighbor, made another new friend, and was still able to drive to the grocery store, the doctor, and the laundromat.

Aunt Gertie lived happily in the gingerbread house for five years. Toward the end of that time, she had to give up driving. I again prayed that God would guide and direct us, but this time, to a home in Arlington where it would be easier for us to help her get groceries and take care of her medical needs. Again, He answered by providing an apartment on South West Street near my office in Arlington.

On the day we moved Gertie into town, I closed the door on the little gingerbread house for the last time with a sense of sadness. For the past five years, that little house had served as a constant reminder to me of God's faithfulness. In closing the door, however, I realized we were also opening another door on South West Street. I knew I could trust God to continue to provide for Gertie's future as He had so faithfully provided for her in the past—but at times when my faith is weak, I enjoy driving past the little gingerbread house on Garcia Lane for encouragement.

> *Not only had God provided the specific needs I had requested... He had also provided extra blessings.*

Honey Bun Surprise

 **Laura Taylor** is a prodigal daughter rescued by the King of Kings. She and her husband reside in beautiful South Carolina, where they own and operate a martial arts school. She enjoys training in martial arts, teaching women's self-defense, visiting the beach with her husband, and spending time with her sons.

The last few teardrops leaked onto my pillowcase.

Please, God. I don't know what to do. We need groceries. I don't want to worry my parents by asking for money again. They already worry so much. I'm fresh out of ideas, and almost out of hope. Help me to trust You.

The alarm blared, dragging me into the day. Heavy-hearted, I climbed out of bed, clinging to the fragile hope that God's answer would come quickly. Across the hallway, little whispers erupted into a cascade of giggles. Older brothers stirred, their voices overlapping as Ryan groaned, "I'm awake!" and Andy grumbled, "Quit jumping on my bed!"

Laughter spilled into the quiet morning, tugging at

the corners of my mouth until my heart lightened. My fragile hope grew stronger as I smiled.

I know You'll come through for us, Father.

My four amazing boys filled my life with wonder, messes, and adventure. I wouldn't trade it for anything in the world. However, I often worried about how to provide for them while waiting for child support to be finalized. Although I taught at a small Christian school, my annual salary registered below the poverty line.

Give me the strength to face them with a smile. Shield their innocent eyes from my anxiousness. And, about the groceries, Father? Help, please.

By God's goodness and strength, the woodpecker of worry silenced its incessant pecking at my heart. God would make a way.

"Who's up for peanut butter stars for breakfast?"

Two little voices piped up, "Me! Me!" Two teenage voices grumbled something about it being too early to eat.

I placed a few slices of bread on the table and dug around to find the cookie cutter. Evan clambered onto the counter to grab the peanut butter from the cabinet.

"Whoa, Mommy! It's empty in here. Do ya think I could hear my echo?"

In wide-eyed wonder, Evan peeked his head inside the empty cabinet, cupped his hands around his mouth, and hollered, "Hello . . . Hello . . ."

I stifled the taunting temptation to worry and silently prayed again for help. Over the last three months, God proved Himself mighty in meeting so many needs. I wouldn't cave in to doubt now.

Lord, You own the cattle on a thousand hills. I just need a few days' worth of groceries—enough to get us through until payday. Father, You are good. You are our Provider. Your Word says nothing is too hard for You.

My mouth rehearsed those truths all morning. Would God come through, or wouldn't He? I wanted to believe. I even imagined ways God might work His miraculous provision.

I recalled reading countless stories about mysterious envelopes appearing just in time, containing the exact amount of money needed. Perhaps this was how God would answer my prayer. Maybe one day, I'd write one of those stories.

My stomach turned a somersault when I heard the mail truck rumble to a stop. Giddy, I strode to the mailbox, convinced the answer to my prayer would be inside. The metal door creaked open, and I peeked inside.

I couldn't believe my eyes. I closed the door and took a deep breath. I opened it again, slowly, certain I'd see God's provision smiling at me. Nothing but a hollow metal container stared back.

What about the prayers I prayed? What about how I trusted God as our Provider? I slammed the mailbox shut, frustrated with my situation and with God. It isn't a holy or righteous thing to admit, but it's true. I needed a way to feed my boys. Evidently, a crisp twenty in the mailbox wasn't God's plan.

Father, are You telling me to swallow my pride and call my parents? It's going to worry my mom. You know that, right?

I trudged back to the house. Anxiety churned deep in my stomach as I fumbled with the doorknob. Like the soothing sound of summer rain after a drought, the Holy Spirit whispered, "Wait."

Wait? For what? There aren't any other deliveries coming today.

I shook my head, not certain what God meant. Then, verses from Psalm 62 began to trickle down, watering my weary heart: "My soul, wait silently for God alone. For my expectation is from Him. He only is my rock and my salvation" (Psalm 62:5-6 NKJV).

Father, help me absorb and apply these truths now. You know what we need. Help me to wait on You.

Just as I opened the door, Andy's voice rang out, "Mom, Mrs. Amanda's on the phone."

"Laura, I just got off the phone with a lady in town. Her church is getting ready to renovate its food pantry and needs to clear it out. She's waiting for you."

God heard my cries. He was already answering them while I moaned at the mailbox.

"I'm on my way!"

As I pulled behind the church, an older woman waved me down. Her grin was infectious, and my excitement palpable.

"Oh, I'm so happy to meet you." She extended a welcoming hand. "We've been looking for a family to bless, and I have to have this food out of here by today."

She led me through a small door into a dimly lit room. A musty smell hung in the air. Somber shadows slid along shelves as if the room itself shared my sinking spirits.

"We are so excited! A local businessman agreed to build us a new pantry and fill it with food. He said we must clear all this food out first."

Her hand reached for a fistful of plastic bags.

"Honey, you go ahead and fill these up!"

I moved toward a shelf holding flour, baking soda, and sugar bags. I reached for a bag of flour as her voice rang out, "Ooh, no, honey! Not those. We had a rodent problem. Mice chewed through lots of boxes and bags. Look-y here."

She pointed behind the bags to layers of mouse droppings, tiny trails of sugar, and floured mouse tracks. The pocket-sized poachers carried away more than pantry items. The remaining crumbs of my optimism disappeared as well.

The woman expressed deep gratitude to me for coming to take this stuff off her hands and excitedly explained how nice their new pantry would be. She guided me around piles of mouse poo and mousetraps as she filled each bag with canned goods and boxes of sweets.

The gloomy room, musty odor, and mouse droppings weren't exactly the experience I had envisioned. I tried hard not to show my disappointment.

Father, help me to be a gracious receiver.

I thanked her for her kindness and headed home. When I pulled up, the boys bounded out the back door and rushed to unload the groceries from the car.

"Mommy, can we have a snack now?" Ethan jumped

up and down with excitement.

They scanned several boxes of sweet treats. Ryan reached for the honey buns, a family favorite. His brothers all decided they wanted honey buns, too. The sound of the crinkling paper opening made my heart smile.

"Yuck! Ugh!" Ryan bent over the trash can and spit out a wad of honey bun.

"What's wrong?"

"Mom, it tastes bad."

"Maybe it's just an off-brand . . . ."

The sound of Andy gagging stopped me mid-sentence. I snatched the honey buns from Evan and Ethan's hands before they could take a bite. The boys stood silent; confusion clouded their faces.

I turned the box over to inspect the expiration date: October 2007. Almost three years had passed since the "use by" date. I looked at the cans and boxes piled on the counter. As I checked each expiration date, my hope began to expire, too.

Every can, every box, every container—no less than two years expired.

Deflated

Hurt.

Defeated.

Hopeless.

What am I going to do now, Father? What do I tell my boys?

"The truth." His gentle voice encouraged:

> Tell them I'm a good Father Who only gives good gifts. I never give second-best or expired leftovers, and I expect my children to give good gifts to others, too. Explain that not all givers reflect My heart. I want you to understand that the real gift today is the lesson. It's a lesson I want you and your sons to carry throughout your lives. Let them talk to you about today. Encourage them to talk with Me. Tell them the parable of the widow who gave her last mite. Remind them I am bigger than any problem they will ever face.

We settled in with peanut butter sandwiches and popcorn for dinner and read the parable. We talked about what it means to be givers who reflect God's heart and how to love our neighbors as ourselves.

Little Ethan looked at me in childlike innocence and whispered, "Mommy, the lady who gave us that old food must not love herself very good. Can we pray for her tonight?"

So, we did.

Right after we finished praying, there was a knock on the back door. Somehow, Amanda heard about the food pantry disaster. She wasted no time showing up with arms full of groceries.

Bags bulged with canned goods, fruit, and fresh veggies. Two boxes of honey buns peeked out of the top of a bag. The boys erupted into cheers. The crinkling wrappers of the fresh honey buns and ripples of laughter were the sounds of God's goodness—a tender Father who delights in surprising His children.

> *"Tell them I'm a good Father Who only gives good gifts."*

Later that night, I thought about the honey bun surprise and wept again as I drifted off to sleep. Only this time, I wept tears of joy.

The Mysterious Midnight Ride

 Reverend Benjamin Santiago was born in Mayagüez, Puerto Rico, in September 1954. One of ten siblings, he moved to the United States at the age of nine and was raised in Delaware before eventually settling in Hartford, Connecticut. With over 45 years in ministry, Reverend Santiago has dedicated his life to serving others and spreading the Gospel. In 1993, he founded New Dimension Christian Center, where he continues to serve faithfully as Senior Pastor. He and his wife, Aida, have five grown children and 15 beloved grandchildren.

That night is etched into my memory as if it happened yesterday. It was 1980, and I was 25 years old. Earlier that day, I had bought a used car in Wilmington, Delaware. I lived in New Castle, just fifteen or twenty minutes down the highway. I was excited to finally have a car of my own, even if it wasn't anything fancy.

Around 1 a.m., I was driving home on the highway, the air bitterly cold—about five degrees, with a windchill that pushed it well below zero. That kind of cold bites through your clothes and settles into your bones.

Then I heard it.

Bum. Bum. Bum.

That rhythmic thudding sound a tire makes when it gives out. I pulled off to the shoulder, heart sinking. A flat tire. *No problem,* I thought. *I'll just change it and be on my way.* I opened the trunk, found the spare, but no jack. I had just bought the car and hadn't thought to check for one.

The cold was unbearable. I had a scarf, but I wasn't dressed for the weather—no thermal pants and definitely not enough layers. I knew I couldn't stay in the car. I might freeze. So I did the only thing I could: I started walking toward the next exit, scarf tied tightly around my head to protect what little I could from the icy wind.

Ten minutes into that walk, the cold became unbearable. My body started to feel numb, and my hope was draining fast. I was alone on a dark stretch of highway, with no idea how far I'd have to walk. That's when I prayed the most desperate prayer I've ever said: *Lord, help me.* That was it. Just those three words. A cry from the depths of my soul.

Not even a minute later, I heard the hum of a car slowing behind me. A brown limousine—an older model, elegant, with beige interior—pulled up alongside me and stopped. I wasn't hitchhiking. I hadn't waved or signaled. I was just walking. "Wow," I whispered. "Who stops for a stranger at this hour?"

I approached the passenger side. The window lowered, and I saw a young woman behind the wheel. She looked about my age—maybe 25 or 30. Blonde and beautiful, she smiled gently, as if she already knew me.

"What happened?" she asked.

"I had a flat tire," I explained, "and I don't have a jack."

"Where are you going?" she asked.

"New Castle."

"Hop in," she said. "I'll give you a ride."

I hesitated only for a second. The warmth pouring from her car was too inviting to resist. I got in.

It was the most luxurious car I'd ever been in—comfortable, warm, almost otherworldly. As we drove, I told her the story of how I had just bought the car that day, how the tire popped, and how I had a spare but no jack. She didn't offer to go back and help change the tire. She didn't mention calling for help. She just kept driving. "It's five degrees," she said at one point. "So cold tonight."

We talked, though I can't recall all that was said. It felt natural, like I was talking to someone I had known for years. I wasn't even paying attention to the route.

There were no phones and no GPS. I never gave her my address—but she drove straight to my house.

Only once she pulled up in front did it dawn on me: *How did she know where to go?* I hadn't told her the street. I hadn't pointed out turns. All I had said was "New Castle." Yet here we were, parked in front of my house.

I thanked her, stepped out, and closed the door. "You're welcome," she said, and just like that—she was gone.

As her car disappeared down the street, something clicked in my mind. *She came right after I prayed. She drove me to my exact house without ever asking for directions.* That's when I realized: she wasn't just a good Samaritan. She was sent.

I believe with everything in me that God answered my cry for help and sent me an angel that night. The cold had become too much. I was convinced I wouldn't make it walking any farther, but I wasn't alone. The Lord saved me.

> I never gave her my address—but she drove straight to my house.

It's been over four decades since that night, but I've never forgotten it. I've shared the story with friends, family, anyone who would listen—not just because it's miraculous, but because it reminds me that when we cry out to God, He listens. Even on the side of a highway, at one in the morning, in the freezing cold.

"You Want to Eat at Braum's"

Dr. Ron Faulk is a retired professor and former jail and prison chaplain who now pastors a small rural church near Tryon, Oklahoma. In 2023, to commemorate the church's 100th anniversary, he published *History of a Small Church*, a work preserving its meeting notes and highlighting the vital role of small congregations in shaping America's faith.

One summer, when I was working as a professor, dean, and accreditation director for a small Catholic liberal arts university in Oklahoma, the university president asked me to join a team at a higher education tech conference in San Jose, California. I agreed but asked him if I could drive out instead of fly. He consented.

A change of scenery would be nice. I was tired—not only physically but mentally and spiritually. This was also a time when the Holy Spirit was very active in my life, so I looked forward to extended quiet time on the drive.

The conference was decent, as conferences go. Afterward, I headed back home via I-80 to visit my son, who lives in Pocatello, Idaho. From there, the drive home would be about two days.

I drove through Emigrant Gap towards the sun rising over Nevada. I like to drive in the West, across its purple mountains and great plains, where you can see a long way, through high, colorful deserts and fertile valleys with the smell of fresh-cut hay. Often in midsummer, huge hammer-headed thunderstorms loom in the distance. In a quiet truck on a lonely road, with beauty and space all around, is a good place to pray, to call on the Lord, and to feel His presence. As the psalmist says, "[A] day in your courts is better than a thousand elsewhere" (Psalm 84:10a ESV).

With great expectation, I left Pocatello early in the morning and set my mind to pray and meditate. But, alas, thoughts began to crowd out my attention on the Lord. I would start to pray, thoughts would intervene, then the same thing, over and over. I could not keep my spiritual focus. It was so aggravating. I did everything I could to focus my attention on the Father, Jesus, Scripture, or anything spiritual, but I was met with a constant battle. For ten straight hours, my mind continued slipping away, and I was unable to master my thoughts. By the end, I was very tired.

When I made it to eastern Colorado, I pulled my Toyota Tacoma into a roadside rest area. As usual on long trips, I had packed a cardboard box with food in it: bread, peanut butter, jelly, tuna fish, cheese, chips, fruit roll-ups, and cookies. I also had a small ice chest with Gatorade, lemonade, and tea (I don't like carbonated drinks). I took my time with a simple dinner, enjoyed the landscape, and watched the night rise from the east. Then I curled up in the sleeping bag in the bed of my truck. It was June, but nights in the high plains are cool enough to make outside sleeping comfortable.

I got up early, hoping that today I could finally rest in the Lord. After eating a small breakfast, I headed into the sun and started praying . . . . The same thing happened. For hours, I wrestled with conflicts and slipperiness in my head. At this point, I was numb and weary. With a blunt mind, I gripped the steering wheel as I traveled over the rolling hills of western Kansas under hot, empty skies.

Suddenly, I heard a clear, distinct voice. It said, "You want to eat at Braum's." Startled, I jerked my head up. I thought to myself, *What do you mean, "I want to eat at Braum's?"* I wondered if I had unconsciously said it or dreamed it. No, I heard it clearly; there was no mistake.

I have heard voices before (I don't tell that to everyone), and I always test and compare them. I am, after all, an empiricist, reluctant to believe anything I cannot directly experience. As I usually do, I thought carefully about what I had just experienced. It was a male voice, midrange in pitch. It was straightforward, factual, not very inflected. It was what I call "voiceless speech." If someone had been sitting next to me, I doubt he or she would have heard it, even though it was quite loud to me.

The Lord, or more likely an agent of the Lord, has spoken to me before. The voice is always the same: calm, factual, direct, easy to understand, male, and not very inflected. By that I mean the pitch is difficult to pin down. It certainly is not robotic, but it lacks the emotional tone of an ordinary human voice. It is also hard to tell which direction it comes from. He says what He says in the shortest, most efficient way possible.

"Okay," I muttered to myself, still feeling a bit perturbed. "I am not sure what the deal is, but in any case, I have not seen a Braum's in the two weeks since I left the central U.S., so this is crazy!" A minute or two later, I rolled to the top of another round hill, and there on the side of the road was a large billboard advertising

"Braum's—Next Exit."

I began to get excited, thinking, *Hey, the Lord wants me to do something!* Maybe there is someone in Braum's I need to witness to, or maybe someone in the parking lot needs help.

I knew the Lord even as a six-year-old, though I had many misconceptions about Him. It was unfortunate that I did not have good spiritual advice at that age; it would have saved me a lot of dumb mistakes and grief. The first time I heard loudly, clearly, and dramatically from the Lord—or an agent of the Lord—I was twenty-one. After that, I heard Him only a few rare times, until I turned forty and was "called." From then on, I began to hear from Him more often. At the time of this event, I was fifty or so.

Over the decades, I've learned that *every* time I try to figure out why the Lord is asking me to do something, or what the results might be, I am wrong. Often, very wrong. I have good analytic skills, and that is how I make my living, but they don't help me foresee the results of God's instructions. Still, I can't resist trying to figure out the Lord. I just have to remember that I will be wrong. This is an ongoing lesson, and I am a slow learner.

Within minutes, I took the exit to Braum's, crossed

over the interstate, and drove a half mile to the store. In the parking lot, I waited for the Lord to point someone out, or at least to see if someone needed help. Nothing. So I walked into the store, got in line (this was around lunch), and gave my order while closely examining the staff. Nothing. Even as I got my food and sat down, all the while scanning the customers—nothing.

> *I've learned that every time I try to figure out why the Lord is asking me to do something, or what the results might be, I am wrong.*

Somewhat disappointed, I found a sunny spot and slowly ate lunch. As I sat there, I slowly realized that I was pretty relaxed. I felt better. Maybe the voice, which I assume was from the Lord, was trying to tell me something simple—like a lunch break at Braum's would do me good. The Lord usually has more important things on His itinerary than that, but, after all, I am the apple of His eye, right?

I strolled out to my truck and headed back to the interstate. Near the on-ramp, I saw a tall, stooped old man trying to hitch a ride. I immediately knew: *this* was what the Lord wanted me to do—pick him up. The old man had been a bit behind me, and the Lord needed to slow me down.

I cannot remember his name, but the man was in his seventies. He lived by hitchhiking up and down the interstate, going to various jobs along the Kansas I-70 homeless grapevine. His pack with bedding and extra clothes had been stolen, so he had nothing—not a toothbrush nor a change of socks. He had heard that a jeans manufacturer in Wichita would give a free pair of jeans to those in need. He was quiet and humble—not the complaining kind. A normal guy, down on his luck and doing the best he could. We visited on the drive to Wichita; then I dropped him off where he asked and gave him a small amount of money.

I was pleased with myself. I had heard from the Lord and did what He wanted! My exhaustion was gone. I felt good. I turned these things over in my mind pleasantly for many miles. But this was not the end of the story.

Suddenly, the truck began to misfire. I immediately knew what was wrong. I had forgotten to get gas! I am not the kind of guy who runs out of gas. In fact, this is the only time in my now longish life that I remember it happening. I started coasting, and behold, just ahead of me was the exit to a rest area. My truck stopped well off the interstate. I was very annoyed but happy to get my truck off the highway. I got out, and about a hundred yards away in front of the rest station was a station wagon with a middle-aged guy leaning against it.

I really do not like to ask for help. I like to be self-sufficient. However, I do like to help others. I carry a tow strap in my truck to pull cars out of ditches in bad weather. Doesn't the Lord say it is better to give than to receive? In the present situation, however, I had no choice. Sheepishly, I walked up to the guy and asked if he could give me a ride to a gas station. "Sure, buddy," he said. About two miles down the road, we found one. I borrowed a container, got gas, and the good Samaritan drove me back. The truck started easily.

In the middle of a crisis, I do not reflect much. But as I sat in my truck with enough gas to get to the station, I began to think about what just happened. It was highly unlikely to be a coincidence. The lessons grew reasonably clear. One, the Lord can make me forget to fill up if He wants to, just as He can let me run out of gas in a convenient place. Two, I really am not that self-sufficient, and I should always rely on the Lord. Three, maybe there is a bit of pride in not wanting to be helped. Four, I shouldn't get inflated because "I" helped someone out. It is God's grace that allows me to help or be helped by others. Finally, the people being helped might even be spiritually stronger than me. Who is helping whom?

With enough gas in the tank, home was about three hours away. As soon as I got back on the highway, I began to pray, and nothing interfered. The Spirit was strong. My focus was good—no slipping away. For the next three hours, it was "nice and easy" with the Lord, and it was very good.

The Faithfulness of God to Speak

Tamara J. Wanner won the 2025 Word Award (Canadian-wide) for contemporary Christian fiction for her debut novel, *Rainbow Baby: Unravelled by Loss.* It honours families who experienced a pregnancy loss and gives voice to a silent grief. Her current work-in-progress echoes her journey with infertility. She shares her husband's photography and encouraging words through her blog at legacyreimaged.com. Bill and Tamara have two adopted children which have flown the nest.

"You are Mine and I am yours, and I will never let you go."

I stood in stunned silence after my pastor removed his hands from my ears. The security I craved found me with those words that echoed in my heart. As a child, fear crippled me. School gifted me with the ability to read, and reading provided an escape and a refuge from the cruelties of recess. Safety resided in staying hidden, not choosing a distinct path but cowering in the middle. That August day in 1991, I began to walk in confidence that God wanted to talk to me and show me the path to take each day.

My uncle Rusty called them "God-nudges." For me, God's voice showed up in a song, a passage of Scripture, an idea that wouldn't go away, or a person's name, and sometimes in a dream He'd sent. Sometimes He spoke through other people, but He never failed to let me know that I was His and He'd never let me go. Whether a season of pain and loss or a season of joy and gain, the bedrock of belonging to Him steadied me. These next three stories speak to the new confidence those words produced.

Faithful Guidance into Ministry

One more semester of university remained after that August day. I signed up for a children's conference where the main speaker, Dian Layton, challenged us to remember that children do not receive Holy Spirit Junior or follow a Jesus Junior. How would we train them in light of that understanding? The morning before I drove south to Regina, where the conference was, I felt a nudge to take a resume and offer to serve Dian, free of charge, in any way

> *He never failed to let me know that I was His and He'd never let me go.*

she needed. I obeyed.

Two months later, she asked me to serve as a nanny for her young children while she worked in tandem with her curriculum partner, Jan Sherman. I said, "Yes." I participated in ministry with her in Washington, D.C., New Jersey, and Pennsylvania. She talked about praise and speaking in tongues as a way to strengthen the inner spirit. I had asked for that gift of tongues many times before, but one night in the hotel room, while she spent time with her boys, God gave me what I asked. That gift carried me through many dark moments. It enabled me to intercede when I had no idea how to pray.

At the end of the time with Dian, I had a decision to make: Would I carry on working with her, or would I go back to Saskatchewan? I sensed the Lord say that He would bring me into my calling regardless of the location. At the eleventh hour, two weeks before school began, I accepted a position as a kindergarten teacher at the Saskatoon Christian School. What a fantastic place to encourage children's growth in their relationship with Jesus!

Faithful Guidance into Marriage

God sent me a ring the summer after my serious

boyfriend broke up with me. Not a ring for me to wear, but a man's wedding ring. I won it in a raffle supporting pro-life. It came when I had no job and no idea what lay in my future. The ring gave me confidence that marriage was God's intention for me.

Two years later, my husband, Bill, walked into my life for the first time (according to me). A 10-minute distance to home became an hour and a half. A friend told me that Bill was serious about marriage in the first month of our relationship. After we got engaged, we traveled to meet his dad, Paul. Paul handed us this beautiful carving of a rose held between two praying hands. What's the significance? Two years earlier, while a friend prayed for me, he saw a picture of me as a crystal rose. What a beautiful confirmation God gave to the two of us that day.

Four years earlier, at a Rick Joyner/John White conference, Bill adjusted my microphone as I prepared to sing on the worship team. As he did so, he got an impression that I would be his wife one day. In the following years, I had supper with his sister and brother-in-law and taught his nieces and nephews. He adjusted the microphone for me at different weddings where I played flute or sang many times after that, but God blinded my eyes until just the right time.

Faithful Guidance Through Seasons of Farming

A year later, we'd gone to my parents' farm to help with the harvest. Bill turned to me and said that if we ever get the chance to farm, we should do that. I'd had the same thought earlier that day. The next day, Dad and Mom asked each of their children whether they'd like to farm with them because a friend's farm was available to us. Bill and I answered yes. One year later, we called our new venture "Jireh Farms Ltd." We knew that only God could provide for us since we had no experience or training.

We'd written down that we'd love to contribute wealth to God's Kingdom at the end of one of our marriage Bible studies we'd done in the city. Boy, were we in for a surprise that first year. Drought and hail decimated our crops. We both found jobs in other fields, in order to pay bills and put food on the table.

The next spring in 1999, I sat before the Lord, and He gave us Psalm 65:

> You care for the land and water it; you enrich it abundantly. The streams of God are filled with water to provide the people with grain, for so you have ordained it. You drench its furrows and level its ridges;

> you soften it with showers and bless its crops. You crown the year with your bounty, and your carts overflow with abundance. The grasslands of the desert overflow; the hills are clothed with gladness. The meadows are covered with flocks and valleys are mantled with grain; they shout for joy and sing. (Psalm 65:9-13 NIV)

We saw abundance that year and provision for all of our needs, including a full-time teaching position. God gave Bill different dreams to prepare us for each farming season ahead. Some years we bought extra crop or hail insurance; other years we invested in machinery or rented more land.

Did all our 23 years of farming resemble the one of abundance? No. Did God call us to trust Him to carry us through each season? Yes. Could we rely on previous God-nudges? No, we had to trust Him for new leading, each and every moment. So, when the two-week pause came in March of 2020, I felt clear leading to say to my husband, "You are released from farming. This is our last year." Other circumstances influenced our decision to leave our small town and step into something new.

In June, the Lord woke me up with a dream about there being "peace in the battle." He gave me a song about being still and watching Him work out all the details. My husband had his best year that year with no machinery breakdowns. He completed the harvest early. The Lord gave my husband a devotional that confirmed that even though we'd miss the valley view, it was the right time to move on.

As we journeyed through the process of selling our company, supporting our daughter, and waiting on surgery for my husband, we rested in an ocean of grace. The Lord gave us confirmation about moving to Moose Jaw through our sister-in-law and our dear neighbor. Each house-hunting weekend ended in unease, but we located a church to attend in Moose Jaw. The weekend of our daughter's birthday led us to an acreage with a heated shop for Bill. We drove onto the lot and, collectively, the peace of having found our new home settled on each of us. We'd dismissed the ad four months earlier, but God's timing proved His faithfulness once again.

Throughout our 29 years of marriage, God led us faithfully—and He continues to do so. Keep listening!

A Mentor's Quiet Legacy: Character Over Gifting

 **Mark Sterns** is a ministry representative with The Voice of the Martyrs. As an aviapreneur with decades of experience in C-suite and organizational governance, he is also passionate about core values that bridge marketplace and ministry to shape culture. Connect with him at mark.sterns@gmail.com.

"I may have to save a life someday."

It was not the answer I expected, but knowing Bob Miranda, I should not have been surprised. Like the old E.F. Hutton stockbroker TV commercial, when Bob spoke, people listened.

That day, I had asked Bob about his morning exercise. Under relentless coaxing, he reluctantly shared that he had run three miles, then did forty-five chin-ups. Forty-five?! I had not done that many in my whole life! He subjected his sixty-one-year-old body to his will and ran stadium steps to finish his workout.

"Why do you work out, Bob?" I asked. I knew it was

not to look good. Perhaps it was to feel good or stay healthy. "I might have to save a life someday," he replied.

Mine was not the only life he impacted. USAF Lt. Col. and F-16 fighter pilot Will Vaughn wrote, "He was unquestionably the softest-spoken, yet most powerful leader who has ever influenced my life; his life was the closest representation of Christ's life that I have witnessed. His life and words continue to be an encouragement to me."

I met Bob when he was a retired FAA Aviation Inspector, the only one to oversee eight different commercial airlines, including Braniff International and Southwest Airlines. The former U.S. Air Force reconnaissance pilot in Vietnam came to help us start a Boeing 737 airline. We accomplished airline certification in record time and in exhilarating fashion.

Shortly after, however, exhilaration faded, and I lost my job as president of the company I had helped turn into a Boeing 737 training powerhouse. Escorted out of my office, it was another low point in a string of personal and financial devastations that left my family nearly destitute.

Yet, I remember laughing most of the way home. I scattered coins from my car across the porch for my boys to find, joyful, not only because I was free of a toxic environment, but because I had passed a test I'd failed once before. This time, God had given me a coach.

The company brought Bob in to help start an airline. What we got in return was a legacy of character that would reshape my future startup company and my life.

Bob wasn't a large man, but he cast a giant shadow. He used to say that nature gave him a low profile. He did not seek place or position. Indeed, I don't remember going through a door with him where Bob did not insist that I go first.

Bob and I were fired on the same day because we wouldn't compromise our integrity. In the wreckage of that morning, I didn't lose everything. I gained something more important: a best friend and a model of the values I would build my life, and eventually my company, around.

In the valleys of life, you don't just gain clarity. You gain conviction. Clarity and conviction gained in the valleys shape your values.

Bob showed me that gifting is good, but character is greater. I watched him live it. He wasn't flashy or loud. He was steady. When our startup company later began training some of the world's most gifted pilots—Blue Angels, Thunderbirds, NASA astronauts, and even former flight crews for every U.S. president since Reagan—Bob's influence kept us grounded in more than just technical skill.

He reminded us daily that technical proficiency was never enough.

One moment in particular remains etched in my memory. Right after we celebrated the graduation of our first student, we got the worst news: Bob had died in a Boeing 737 crash in El Salvador. It was a devastating loss.

He traveled to Central America many times, serving countries whose airlines were barred from U.S. airspace for safety reasons. Riding with the pilots on that final flight, a perfect storm of miscommunication, cultural deference in the cockpit, and an intense thunderstorm led to a tragedy that

> *In the valleys of life, you don't just gain clarity. You gain conviction.*

took 65 lives. Bob's body was the only one never recovered, but I knew where to find him. He remained in me, in every student and instructor who passed through our doors, in every word I spoke over new classes, and in the values we upheld.

Bob's family gave me his aviation library. Inside was a copy of a letter he had written to the CEO of TACA Airlines, returning the pay for his first day. He didn't want to accept money that might "scandalize" their relationship. He hadn't come for the check. He came to serve.

Bob embodied the creed in his 1955 Air Force leadership manual:

> Any leader must be technically proficient in both his specialty and leadership techniques. But technical proficiency alone is not enough. Before a man can lead others, he must learn to control himself. He must be a mature man with moral principles, standards to live by, and an aim and purpose in life.

Bob had all of that, and he left it with us.

When we started Higher Power Aviation, I quoted that very passage to every incoming class. I wanted them to know that no matter how much gifting we possessed, our character was more important.

The Apostle Paul spoke of gifting in 1 Corinthians 13:1-3 (ESV):

> If I speak in the tongues of men and of angels but have not love, I am a noisy gong or a clanging cymbal. And if I have prophetic powers, and understand all mysteries

and all knowledge, and if I have all faith, so as to remove mountains, but have not love, I am nothing. If I give away all I have, and if I deliver up my body to be burned, but have not love, I gain nothing.

In verses 4-8, he compares the highest gifting with the character of love and declares it is worth nothing:

> Love is patient and kind; love does not envy or boast; it is not arrogant or rude. It does not insist on its own way; it is not irritable or resentful; it does not rejoice at wrongdoing, but rejoices with the truth. Love bears all things, believes all things, hopes all things, endures all things. Love never ends. As for prophecies, they will pass away; as for tongues, they will cease; as for knowledge, it will pass away.

Paul finally concludes in 1 Corinthians 13:13:

> So now faith, hope, and love abide, these three; but the greatest of these is love.

When gifting fades away, character remains. In its highest form, character is love and is what endures.

Bob taught me that you lead with your life before you lead with your résumé. He taught me to be the kind of man who returns the paycheck on the first day—because the job isn't about what you get but what you give.

I don't know how many lives Bob saved. I do know mine was one of them. His story—his steady, quiet, integrity-filled story—became the cornerstone of ours. We built a company on it. We built a life on it.

And we never forgot that the smallest man in the room often casts the longest shadow.

Editor's Note: While many stories in this collection reflect how God reveals His presence and faithfulness through personal circumstances, this story reminds us of another way God speaks: through the lives of others. Sometimes the clearest reflection of His truth comes in the steady integrity, character, and quiet witness of a friend or mentor. As we see in Scripture, God often uses people to model the values He calls us to live by, giving us flesh-and-blood examples of love, humility, and faithfulness. Through Bob's life and influence, we are reminded that God's Word is not only read but also lived out—and sometimes His greatest lessons come through the faithful shadows cast by those who walk before us.

The Power at Work Within Us

Kari Ingram lives in Birmingham, Alabama, where she is currently working on her first novel—a story about narcissistic abuse. When she's not busy with her grandkids or working on her book, you can find her hitting the trails and soaking up the great outdoors. You can connect with her at KariIngram.com.

Brad walked into the office humming a Toby Mac tune. "GOOD morning!" he sang out, dropping his backpack into the chair next to his desk before turning toward mine. "You doin' okay today?"

I opened my mouth to say something but quickly closed it again. If I let the words out, there would be no going back, and I couldn't make sense of things just yet. "Yeah, I'm fine."

With a slight cock of his head, he raised an eyebrow. "You sure?"

Ugh! Could I keep nothing hidden? My expressions and the tone of my voice seemed to betray me, no matter how hard I tried to keep my thoughts and feelings under wraps.

"Yep." I turned quickly toward my screen, pretending to be engrossed in my inbox. *Let it drop. Let it drop. Let it drop.*

Brad sat down and opened his laptop.

Thank you, God.

I responded to a couple of emails, printed out roll sheets for that night's youth group meeting, and went online to order a couple of things for the upcoming retreat. I had been the Administrative Assistant for the youth department for about six months, and loved it! Brad was great to work with, and I enjoyed getting to know the rest of the church staff better—not to mention the kids! Teenagers were a hoot!

But . . .

Things were beginning to feel . . .

Different.

I couldn't explain it exactly. I had this unnerving sense that things were about to change—that God was up to something. I just didn't know what.

Two weeks prior, I had met with the worship pastor. His administrative assistant was moving away, and the position was opening. My unease had prompted me to consider a move to that position. Was that what I was sensing? We talked for a while—an informal interview. The position was mine if I wanted it. After praying about it, I turned the position down. It just didn't feel right.

The disquiet persisted.

The pastors had been meeting daily for the last few weeks, seeking God's direction for the church in the new year, coming up with a list of things they would "pound the table about"—those things they discerned were crucial to the fulfillment of God's purposes for our church. Brad was not only my boss—he was my friend. He would often come into the office after one of those meetings and bounce ideas off me, eager to hear my opinions.

A few days earlier, he had come in talking about assimilation. "We really need someone to do assimilation. I could see you doing something like that." Blah, blah, blah. He spoke the rest of his words into the air.

My mind had zeroed in on one word. Assimilation? What on earth is assimilation? Isn't that something from Star Trek?

My curiosity took hold, and I did a quick internet search for "assimilation" as it related to the church.

Interesting. Assimilation is about connecting people.

Welcoming guests. Leading them into church membership. Helping members become fully engaged in the life and ministry of the church.

Well, that answered that! That was definitely NOT me! I much preferred staying on the periphery of church activity. Get in. Get out. Don't speak to anyone I don't know. I was much too shy to serve in a position like that. No way. No how.

That night, I barely slept. I awoke repeatedly, thoughts bouncing around my head like pinballs. *What would you do if someone came into the church on Sunday morning and wanted to know which Bible study class they should visit? What would you do if a family visited, and you needed to get a high schooler across the street to the gym, a middle schooler to the other end of the annex, and a toddler upstairs to the nursery? What would you do if a guest told you they really liked the sermon, but the music was too loud? How would you encourage a first-time guest to return the next week?* The questions that peppered my mind were relentless!

The next day, I ordered a book about assimilation. Not that I was interested. I was merely curious. That was all. Inquisitive.

Two days later, the book arrived. I devoured it within

a couple of hours.

God, what are you doing? This isn't me! You know how shy I am! I'm not good at hospitality. I barely talk to people I know, much less those I don't! I'm not a leader. I'm much better at following. You know that. You made me. Besides that, I can't remember my own name half the time. I wouldn't remember a guest's name, and well, wouldn't that be awkward? This is way too far out of my comfort zone. Outside of my gifting. Yes! That's it. It's outside of my spiritual gifting, so this is certainly not something you would want me to do. Right? Right, Lord?

"That's right, My child. It's outside of your gifting."

See? I knew you weren't asking me to do this. It was just a silly idea that got stuck in my head. It didn't mean anything.

"You won't do it. I will."

Yep. That's right. You will do it. You will raise up the right person with the right gifts, and it will be great! The church will really benefit.

"I will do it through you."

Um, come again, Lord? I don't understand. Didn't we just settle this? I don't have the right gifts, the right skill set. You know the right person for the job. Someone who is friendly and outgoing. Someone who loves meeting new people. Someone who has good leadership skills. You know the person already, so, Lord, please speak to that person . . .

"I'm speaking to you."

Uh, Lord? I don't understand.

"You will be obedient. You will trust Me, and I will do the work through you."

But, Lord . . .

"When you do great things with your gifts, people applaud you. When you do things that require gifts and skills you don't have, people applaud Me."

Well, you've got me there. But are you sure I'm the one?

"Try me."

I don't know if Brad saw something on my face or if he caught me staring off into space, but later that morning, he approached my desk again. "Are you sure you're okay? You seem a little preoccupied."

I took a deep breath and let out a loud sigh. "Brad, ever since you mentioned assimilation, it's all I've been able to think about. I can't eat. I can't sleep. I think about it all the time! I think God is telling me something, but I'm not sure what to do with it."

"You need to talk to Jeff."

Jeff was the executive pastor and was in charge of all the day-to-day operations of the church.

"Well, I'm going to the coffee shop to work on my talk for tonight. I'll see you later." Brad grabbed his backpack and headed out the door before I could say anything else.

That was strange. I thought we could at least talk about it a bit. After all, he was the one who started me thinking about this.

Another sigh.

I picked up the phone and dialed the executive pastoral assistant. "Hey, Michelle. I need to talk to Pastor Jeff. Can you put me on his calendar somewhere?" Next week? Next month? Maybe next year?

"Sure! How about 2:00?"

"TODAY???"

"Yeah, he's got some free time this afternoon."

I gulped hard. "Okay. I'll see you later."

I hung up the phone and looked around the youth office, searching for something, anything, that could distract me until 2:00, and noticed the clutter on the shelves. Maybe I could organize!

I jumped up, trying to ignore the doubts that assailed me. *What if you misheard God?* I reached for several games that someone had placed haphazardly on three different shelves. *Do you really think He's going to use you?* Stacking them up neatly, I placed them on the bottom shelf. *Who do you think you are?* I straightened the reams of colored paper. *You don't have what it takes!* I gathered some stray books from the table and shelved them. *Jeff is going to laugh when you tell him.* A bowling ball? Why did we have a bowling ball? *You'll have to quit your job.* I deposited the midnight blue bowling ball into a box in the back corner of the office, out of the eyesight of any youth it might tempt. *You might even have to change churches.*

When I could take the onslaught of thoughts no more, I shut the office door and collapsed into my desk chair. With hands over my face, I cried out, "God, are You sure?"

"Trust Me."

Another deep breath. Another glance at the clock. Five minutes. I could take the long way around to the main building, which housed all the other pastors' offices.

Three and a half minutes later, I arrived at Michelle's desk. "I'll let him know you're here." A quick phone call, and Pastor Jeff opened his door with a beaming smile. "Come on in!"

I took a couple of tentative steps into the office, where Jeff invited me to sit on the maroon loveseat. He settled in the wingback chair across from me. "What's on your mind?"

Ignoring my queasiness, I opened my mouth and allowed the words to tumble out in a jumble of cartwheels and somersaults as I recounted the workings of my mind over the previous few days. Jeff's face gave nothing away as I unloaded my thoughts.

> **"Okay, God, You got me into this! I'm trusting You to do what You do!"**

"I don't know what it means, but there it is."

Pastor Jeff stood. "Okay, well, thanks for sharing your heart. Let me have some time to consider what you've told me, and we'll talk some more next week."

I left the office feeling—I don't know—lighter? Yet still beset by doubts.

God, I did what You told me to do. Can we just get back to normal now? Maybe this was just a test of obedience. You aren't really calling me to a new thing, are You? ARE YOU?

The answer came the following week, when Pastor Jeff called me to his office.

"We would like for you to move out of the youth

office to an office in the main building. Your new title is Director of Assimilation."

I gulped hard in disbelief.

Okay, God, You got me into this! I'm trusting You to do what You do!

Over the next year, God was on display as I successfully learned the names of all 450 church members, tripled the church's guest retention rate, and led an event for over 2,000 members of the community.

> Now to him who is able to do far more abundantly than all we ask or think, according to the power that is at work within us, to him be glory in the church and in Christ Jesus throughout all generations, forever and ever. Amen. (Ephesians 3:20-21 ESV)

My Mary Christmas

Nancy Carolyn Lee is an author and blogger who is passionate about encouraging others through her writing, church ministries, and her job as the parenting director at Willow Network. Nancy lives in the Mohawk Valley in Upstate New York with her husband and small mixed-breed dogs, and she is a proud mother of four young adults and a bonus son. You can find Nancy at InspirationalLee.com and on Amazon.

I brushed away a stray wisp of hair that had fallen out of my ponytail as I fried the last of the calamari, handed the cans of clams to my daughter to open, and started boiling water for the angel hair. I was so excited! I was determined to make this—my mother's last Christmas Eve—the best possible.

Mom had been a part of our Christmas Eve celebrations going way back. In the early years, when my children were young and she was a new widow, we would attend the five o'clock Christmas Eve service at her church, which catered to young children. Then we would go to the shopping center across the street and dine at our favorite buffet. My sister would meet us there with her children and grandchildren, and sometimes my brother would come with his family. The adults would sit around and chat for hours, and the cousins would hang out together and sneak over to the dessert table multiple times.

When the kids had outgrown the children's service, I decided to start our own tradition. My husband is Italian and has fond memories of seafood feasts on Christmas Eve, so I decided to begin the custom with our family.

In the early years, I would fry all the food at home, but I soon realized the prices were so inflated before Christmas that it didn't cost any more to order from a local restaurant. From then on, I would cook a few items myself and order takeout for the rest.

My mother often joined our feasts, unless she was away on a trip to visit one of her other children. After she gave up driving, I would send one of my young adult children to pick her up.

This year was significant.

In August, Mom was diagnosed with brain cancer, and the doctor told us she wasn't expected to make it to Thanksgiving, let alone Christmas. Though Mom was slowing down, she was still managing surprisingly well. As Christmas approached, I was eager with anticipation. I was determined to have my mother over for one last Christmas Eve seafood feast, and I wanted it to be perfect.

I was feeling optimistic about how everything was falling into place. I called my mother in the morning, and she said she was feeling up to coming.

The food was almost done, and the table was carefully set with pink and blue floral china, flatware made of real silver engraved with an "L," and Fostoria crystal goblets, all heirlooms from my mother. A gingerbread house made by my daughter served as the centerpiece.

I was about to hand my daughter the keys to the car to pick up Grandma when the phone rang. My daughter gave me the phone and took over at the stove.

"Hello, Nancy?" It was my mother speaking in a soft, shaky voice. "I am so sorry to disappoint you, but I am just not feeling up to coming to dinner."

"Of course, Mom, I understand," I said, trying not to reveal my disappointment. "I'll come over after we eat and bring you dinner and your gifts."

My son arrived a few minutes later with the take-out. As we sat down at the table and my husband said grace, a tear trickled down my cheek. Even though I was grateful for my family sitting around the table—my husband, my son, my two daughters, and my daughter's boyfriend—I was keenly aware of the empty chair to my right. I politely tried to keep the conversation going, but my mind was distracted, and all I could think about was leaving to check on my mother.

When we finished eating, I packed up a special dinner for my mother—grilled haddock, shrimp, scallops, and angel hair with clam sauce—all gluten-free to accommodate her special diet. Then I grabbed her bag of gifts.

I said goodbye to my family and told them I would serve dessert when I got back.

On the half-hour drive to my mother's apartment, I had time to think. I thought about what Mom had said on the phone. She hadn't said she was disappointed that she couldn't come. She said she was worried about disappointing *me*.

It hit me that my big idea of bringing my mother over for one last perfect Christmas Eve seafood feast was all about me and not about her. Even on one of her better days, it would have been tiring for her.

This made me think about a Bible story not usually

associated with Christmas—the story of Mary and Martha. While Martha was rushing around putting together a meal and complaining that her sister wasn't helping, Mary was sitting at Jesus' feet, hanging on his every word.

My mother didn't need me to be her daughter, Martha, scurrying around and trying to create the ideal occasion. What she needed was for me to be a daughter like Mary, to slow down and simply sit with her.

And what about Jesus? I had to admit that I hadn't taken the time to sit at the feet of Jesus. I was ashamed that my focus had been on myself. I hadn't even asked my mother what she wanted or considered what was best for her. I prayed for God to renew my attitude and to use me to bless my mother on her last Christmas Eve.

> **What she needed was for me to be a daughter like Mary, to slow down and simply sit with her.**

A sense of gratitude washed over me as I realized what an honor it was to welcome the birth of the Christ child—the Savior of the world—one last time with my mother before she would meet Jesus face to face.

When I walked into her apartment, Mom was dozing

on her recliner. I quietly stuffed her stocking with the gifts I brought, tiptoed into her kitchen, and filled the tea kettle. Then I made a small plate of food and set it down on the table beside her. I picked her Bible up off the end table and sat down next to her, sliding my hand into hers. Her eyelids fluttered as she opened her eyes with recognition. "Why, Nancy, you're here," she said as her face lit up with a smile. "You didn't have to come."

I squeezed her hand and smiled back. "There is nowhere else I would rather be," I said.

Beloved

 **Dr. Robert "Bob" Mendonsa** and his wife Julie founded Naomi's Village Children's Home and Cornerstone Preparatory Academy in Kenya, after four medical mission trips to Kijabe. Formerly in private orthopedic practice in Texas, Bob moved his family to Kenya in 2008 after Julie heard a strong call from the Lord to address the orphan crisis there. Today, Bob serves as CEO of Naomi's Village, overseeing administration, intake, program and staff development, and fundraising, under a vision to raise the children of Naomi's Village to become future leaders for Kenya. Connect with Bob through naomisvillage.org.

It almost ended there, in a dark cylindrical shaft, not two feet across and fifteen feet below Earth's sweeter surface.

Floating in raw sewage, the Kenyan baby boy survived because of a simple misunderstanding of buoyancy. By wrapping him in a plastic bag that miraculously trapped air around his tiny newborn frame, his mother unintentionally saved his life.

He had only recently departed one watery milieu

inside her womb, attached and warm, nurtured by every maternal heartbeat—safe. Then, after sensing warm light and hearing voices, he was awakened later by a sudden splash as he landed in human waste, having been dropped down a pit latrine. He now lay confused and alone in a dark hell, an unforgiving vertical tomb with no relief in sight.

Some candles, when lit in storms, blow out quickly before ever brightening any scene.

At least six hours passed in the night from the time the pit latrine had last been used until another woman came to relieve herself. As she positioned herself, she clearly heard crying from the damp hole beneath her. She began screaming in horror at the thought. Baby cries, a human child in need—and how could it have gotten down there, in such a terrible place?

A clamorous crowd quickly surrounded the outhouse, at first unable to accept such news from her without coming to a quiet to hear for themselves. Distant, pained screams welled up from underneath their feet. A flashlight confirmed the truth. Someone caught a glimpse of his flesh, a tiny eye peeking out of the foul darkness now wrapped in fearful suspense.

A man of uncommon bravery stepped forward and

volunteered to go into the pit. Someone found a rope and quickly tied it around his waist. Headfirst he went, fighting the rush of blood to his head, the uncertain darkness, and the sewer gas. Down he crawled, approaching the contents of the latrine, his shoulders scratching against earthen walls on either side. "Pole, pole!—*Slowly!*" he yelled as the infant came into focus.

Angels must have celebrated the moment, as an unwanted baby boy was cradled by his hero and brought skyward, to thrive in the hopeful light of day again. There could have been no worse odds against being rescued, and all the more when he was so utterly helpless and weak. Parallels exist for we who also once lay dirtied, unable to save ourselves, and who were suddenly plucked and brought up to live in the brightest place, full of wonder and solidity. Only God does such things—sends saviors into the bleakest night to rescue the dying.

His first name, given by the hospital in Narok, was Abandoned. Bonface from Naomi's Village (NV) fought back tears as he watched the story on TV that evening, then notified us in Bulgaria, where our family was attending a conference. We encouraged him to take a team to visit the baby. He went the very next day.

NV had never rescued a baby from that town, a full 90 minutes away.

Within a half hour of hearing about this boy, I knew that he was to be called David. Later, we looked up the name and discovered that it meant "beloved," confirming that this was to be the handle that defined his new identity.

Twenty-one days passed, marked by prayers and worries, as he lay in a hospital bassinet undergoing treatment. Premature celebrations arranged and canceled on several days left us wondering. And then he finally came home one sunny Wednesday, as sure as the happy ending of a perfect play.

The NV gates opened, and we smiled and cheered until our faces hurt. We sang and danced, passed him around and kissed him, before sharing his celebration cake. We remembered our own stories and what it felt like to be clean again, to start over with a forever fresh slate in a crowd of the redeemed.

We worshiped God, who finds the hopeless in deep, narrow pits of despair and brings them home to live in wide-open places, full of love and song and purpose. And we did so, aware that even the best of these places is shadowy at times, unable to compare to the home that awaits us on that Day, farther up and brighter still.

Life and color, loving touch, early literacy, healthy attachment, nutrition, and the riches of a giant worldwide family will fill David's future. For the next two years, our baby moms will give him their expert attention, caring for every aspect of his babyhood. There will be those glorious toddler years to follow, bounding around the hallways of Naomi's Village, singing in the dining hall, visiting the beach every December, and opening Christmas gifts with his siblings. He will begin at Cornerstone Preparatory Academy in five years, and we will put a solid stone under every one of his dream steps.

> **We worshipped God, who finds the hopeless in deep, narrow pits of despair and brings them home...**

And perhaps one day, by the grace of God, this beloved boy will stand tall and tell his story to thousands. If so, it will be one that is too awful and too beautiful to be true at the same time, a vivid echo and a reminder of the greatest story ever told.

A Note from the Editors

Torch Runner Books, an imprint of Harris House Publishing, was created to equip Christian authors to fulfill their God-given purpose.

Since our beginning, we've dreamed of creating a collection that highlights the many ways God's light shines in and through His people. *Torchlight Testimonies* is the fulfillment of that dream—a gathering of stories from believers who have witnessed God's faithfulness in both ordinary and extraordinary moments.

We are so thankful to the authors who shared their stories for this collection. We're also thankful for you, dear reader, for embarking through these pages with us. Our hope is that these testimonies have renewed your sense of hope and joy, and maybe even encouraged you to entrust God once again with every part of your life. We also hope they have inspired you to share your own story of God's faithfulness.

All throughout Scripture, the Israelites were reminded to remember God's mighty works and to tell them to the next generation. You have the opportunity to do the same. On the next page, you'll find a simple guide to help you write your own testimony. Whether it's your salvation story, an answer to prayer, a moment of encouragement, or another way you've seen God at work—whatever it is, we encourage you to tell of God's works to those around you, passing on the remembrance of His faithfulness as a light for the generations.

If you'd like, you can share your story with us, too. In the spirit of carrying the torch of testimony forward, we invite you to submit your story for possible publication on our blog or a future anthology. You can learn more at our website: http://torchrunnerbooks.com/share-your-story.

> Oh give thanks to the Lord; call upon his name; make known his deeds among the peoples! Sing to him, sing praises to him; tell of all his wondrous works!
> (1 Chronicles 16:8-9 ESV)

Share Your Testimony

Stories connect people in a way that opens their hearts to hear what you have to say. Here are some tips for sharing your story in a way that honors Christ and encourages someone else.

1. Before Christ (or before faith was real to me)
    a. What was my life like? What struggles, questions, or emptiness did I face?
2. Meeting Christ (the turning point)
    a. How did I first encounter Jesus? What led me to trust Him or make faith personal?
3. Life after Christ (the difference now)
    a. How has my life, perspective, or purpose changed? What hope, peace, or strength do I now experience?
4. Scripture or Truth Anchor (optional)
    a. What verse connects with your story or could you use to encourage others?

5. Invitation/Encouragement

    a. What is one sentence I can share to encourage others to trust God with their story

"They triumphed over him by the blood of the Lamb and by the word of their testimony; they did not love their lives so much as to shrink from death." (Revelation 12:11 NIV)

Adapted from handouts by Rebecca Frederick Lambert from her conference, *Planted: The Revival of You.* Used by permission. Rebecca Frederick Lambert ©2025.

Voice of the Martyrs (VOM) is a Christian, interdenominational nonprofit committed to supporting believers who face persecution around the world. Since its founding in 1967, VOM has worked to deliver practical aid, strengthen persecuted Christians in their faith, encourage Gospel witness in difficult places, and raise global awareness of religious persecution.

All proceeds from this book will be donated to VOM.

Learn more or get involved at
persecution.com

This anthology is an independent project and has not been sponsored, endorsed, or authorized by Voice of the Martyrs.

About Torch Runner Books

Passing the Baton of Faith through the Written Word

At Harris House Publishing, our mission is rooted in helping others share the stories God has placed on their hearts—and that calling has only expanded with our imprint: Torch Runner Books.

Inspired by Psalm 68:11 (KJV), "The Lord gave the word: great was the company of those that published it," Torch Runner Books began as a spark—a personal calling to "publish the word"—and has grown into a movement of authors, each carrying a torch of truth, testimony, and transformation.

Through our hybrid publishing model, we equip writers with the tools, support, and platform they need to boldly step into their calling. Torch Runner Books is more than just an imprint—it's a relay of faith, a passing of the baton from writer to reader, generation to generation. Each book we publish becomes a flame in someone's hands, lighting the way for others to walk more closely with the Lord.

You can support the mission and vision of Harris House Publishing and Torch Runner Books by reading and reviewing our books.

Connect with us at:
harrishousepublishing.com
torchrunnerbooks.com

Your honest review of *Torchlight Testimonies* could help someone else discover it. Search for it on Amazon or Goodreads to leave your review.

God bless you as you run this relay of faith!

www.ingramcontent.com/pod-product-compliance
Lightning Source LLC
Chambersburg PA
CBHW070136080526
44586CB00015B/1716